BEYOND THE RIVERS OF SUDAN

THE PROPHECY AGAINST CUSH

By

ADIER MACH DENG

2016

COPYRIGHT

First Printing: 2016

ISBN 978-0-692-51592-1

52495>

9 780692 515921

www.adierdeng.org

Ordering Information:

Special discounts are available on quantity purchases by corporations, associations, educators, and others. For details, contact the publisher or the author at the above listed address.

U.S. trade bookstores and wholesalers: Please contact author at www.adierdeng.org.

TABLE OF CONTENTS

DEDICATION

It is with utmost sincerity that I dedicate this book to my comrades, compatriots, and believers as well as non-believers who have taken the time to read it. Also, I dedicate this book to the people of Cush (South Sudan), who in my opinion are one of the most hospitable people in the world.

The new generation is at odds with Islamic jihadists' fundamentalism, seeing as the land of Sudan is a medley of Christianity, Islam, and other indigenous animist beliefs. As such, the downtrodden in the land that need support and good cheer are very welcome to read this book; it is to them also that I dedicate it.

ACKNOWLEDGEMENTS

This book is based on real life experience and research conducted between 2012 and 2015. I am grateful for a number of friends and colleagues in encouraging me to start the work, persevere with it, and finally to publish it. I would like to thank my professors, my editor, my creative writing course classmates, and my family without whose help this book would never have been completed.

AUTHOR'S BIOGRAPHY

Adier Mach Deng was born in the village of Dong, Twic East, South Sudan. As a boy raised in this region, he experienced the cruel reality of civil wars, genocide, and massacres through mid-1980 to early 2000. These events were traumatizing, and his life was changed forever. Courage was important and necessary when he was young, and he had no choice but to become brave as this was integral to his survival! While on the run from both the Sudanese government and the splinter rebel group, he had to find safety, because the government's soldiers captured older people and killed or scared the younger people away. He fled and trekked for over 2,500 miles on barefoot, seeking shelter, security, and a place to call home.

After spending nine years as a refugee in Kenya, Adier moved to the United States as part of the so-called "Lost Boys& Girls of Sudan" and the call within became too strong to ignore, so he took action. In 2000, he came to America as a refugee. Here, he obtained his high school diploma from Hudsonville High School, his Bachelor's degree from Aquinas College, Master's degree from the University of Michigan-flint, a second Master's degree from John F. Kennedy University, and anticipating a Doctorate degree from Cal University in California.

In 2005, he was selected for a competitive United States Senate internship where he worked for a law maker, Senator Carl Levin of Michigan.

Adier is a deeply passionate person, especially involving issues relating to Marxism, religion, and humanitarianism. He was raised in the Christian faith, and never misses a chance to share his 'message' with the world, for he sees his mission as the rachis of faith and hope. As the blessed father of a two-year-old son, he is a family man who upholds family principles. He has experienced God's grace.

PREFACE

Known in the deepest reaches of recorded history as the land of "Kush", Sudan is a region that has rested deep in the consciousness of the planet for thousands of years. The ancient Kingdom of Sudan was vast and at one point stretched all the way to the Sinai. This vast empire would change borders and demarcations over the centuries, but over the years one thing that wouldn't change was the passion of the people.

When Sudan first became Christian in the late fifth century, the Sudanese response to Christianity was one of the most enthusiastic in all of Africa, only to be rivaled by the Orthodox fervor of the Ethiopians in the South. And after the rise of Islam and Arab conquest, ideological passion in the region flamed bright once again. This time however the land of Sudan was one that was destined for an ideological split of epic proportions, leaving the north firmly in the camp of Islam, while the South fiercely struggled to keep their non-Muslim identity intact. It is from this ideological struggle that began centuries ago that we can find the roots of the SPLM.

The struggle was always there under the surface, but the true resistance began in earnest when the false flag of freedom had been raised by the United Nations by official decree in 1956. It was this year that it was declared by official UN charter that Sudan was to join the rest of the world of free and independent nations, yet for the disenfranchised south this freedom still remained a remote mystery.

For the people of the oppressed south, this freedom remained elusive and every day survival was the most that the average Sudanese could hope for. John Garang was only 11 years old and already an orphan. The biggest concern of his day was just to make sure that he would live to see another. Announcements from strange faraway places of phantom freedoms would have to wait.

As bad as John Garang's circumstances were however, he was fortunate enough to have others looking after him. Unlike many of his orphaned peers he had a strong backbone of relatives that instilled in him at a young age that he should be educated. They even paid for much of his schooling, an effort that would pay off in the form of an eventual scholarship and opportunity to study in the United States where he would receive a PHD in Agriculture Economics. As fate would have it however, when John Garang returned back to Sudan, being a farmer was just not in the cards for him.

A fate that seemed to have been sealed in 1972 when Jaafar Muhammad and Joseph Lagu signed the Addis Ababa Agreement, an agreement that was supposed to bring peace, but instead brought war. As the entire political landscape began to unravel under Garang's feet any ideas he had of working with the country's agricultural programs were pushed aside as he found himself rushing to join the Sudanese Army to fight what he viewed as an unfair imposition being placed upon the South.

From scholar to soldier he soon attained the rank of Colonel in the military before leaving again, for of all places, Fort Benning George in the United States, where he furthered his military training, having only one goal in his mind the entire time; the full liberation of his people.

When John Garang's second odyssey in the United States drew to a close he came back to the land of his birth for the second time and found that it was in a state of chaos, much worse than he could have imagined. The Dhain Massacre of 1987 had left 3000 South Sudanese dead and the outlook of everyone involved was beyond bleak in its scope. The Islamists were attempting to enforce Sharia law on all of Sudan and were keeping the Southern Sudanese in virtual slavery.

With the cries of his people piercing his ears, John Garang had to do something. That something came in the form of the "Sudan People's Liberation Movement" (SPLM). A group that was formed with nothing less than not only the liberation, but also the complete vindication of a people that had been downtrodden for centuries by an unjust polity in the north. This was the vehicle that Dr. Garang used to bring about the social justice that the people of the south so desperately needed.

THE INTRODUCTION OF ISLAM

The Byzantine Christian church was flourishing in Nubia; Northern Sudan up until the Arabians slowly infiltrated Sudan and spread a wave of Islam into the area, converting many of the people to Islamic fundamentalism. By the time Sudan became independent and the British were forced to withdraw their forces from the land, most of the North, which made up the majority of the population, was Arabic and Islamic by religion.

As soon as the Islamic fundamentalists took over the helm of affairs in the north, they immediately waged war against the predominantly Christian south. Roman missionaries had commenced work in the area beginning in 1842, and both Anglican and Presbyterian missionaries had been present since 1899.

At first, this war appeared to be the product of ethnic and political differences, but by the time the Islamic Fundamentalists declared Sharia law in Sudan, trespassing against peoples' freedom of religion, the real reason for the war became apparent. The Islamists were displeased with the Christianity of South Sudan and they were hell-bent on eradicating from the area any religion that was not Islam. They declared apostasy (the conversion of an individual from Islam to another religion), a capital crime punishable by death.

Under the various military regimes in the Sudan, there was intense persecution of the Christians. The Muslims did not consider the fact that they were by population, more numerous than the Christians, constituting about 62 percent of the population, and animists making up another 22 percent, leaving the remainder to Christianity. They had more or less declared an internal Jihad against South Sudan where the population was densely Christian. Half of Sudan's Christian population was South Sudanese, and these Christians faced massive persecution on many fronts most especially from the Northern Islamic fundamentalists.

This has thus far been an account of the development of the religion and cultures of the Northern Sudanese people with far less been known about the more indigenous Southern Sudanese people who did not have the privilege of having Egypt as neighbors and so having any written history. What is well known about them is that they also slowly embraced Islam and African religions. Soon enough, European colonization swept into Sudan and the British were the colonial masters of the Sudan.

They administered the Northern and Southern provinces separately. While they deemed the North more similar to Egypt as elucidated above, they deemed the more indigenous southern lands to the East African states of Kenya, Uganda and Tanganyika. The North was the more influential sect and they pressured the British (who finally succumbed by 1946) into amalgamating both tribes by way of integration. The Northern elite soon began to hold prominent positions among the people of the Southern Sudan, and the cultural differences especially in language and religion soon irked the Southern Sudanese.

MODERN DAY SUDAN

As the British were withdrawing their colonial powers from East Africa, they hastily amalgamated several areas to create the present day Sudan. Of course, they did this without really caring about the people or the tribes. All they cared about was the geographical locations that were being blended and that it would look good on a map.

In 1956, when independence was granted to this never-before-country, a civil war had been raging for over a year between the northern and southern tribes. It was like handing a bomb to two children who never agreed.

The two areas are always at loggerheads with each other and never really agree on anything from language to traditions, and the British, the 'benevolent' benefactors, placed their independence before them on a platter of gold and simply walked out. Like true and proper children, they squabbled over it. The north was primarily Muslim, and the south, a mixture of Christians and animists.

A handful of fundamentalist Muslim tribes seized control at the end of the colonial era and continued the imperial strategies with a simple singular change – to eliminate the populations and impose Islam and Arab cultures. As the British were withdrawing their colonial powers from East Africa they hastily joined several jurisdictions to create Sudan. The British favored the north but sought water, oil, gold and other resources in the south.

A handful of fundamentalist Muslim tribes seized control at the end of the colonial era and continued the imperial strategies with a single change: eliminate the populations, impose Islam and Arab culture.

In the first war 1.5 million Africans died. There was a hiatus between 1972 and 1983. Then Sharia Law was proclaimed against the south declaring that all Sudanese must convert to Islam or accept pain of death.

Another cause for dispute presented itself when large oil reserves were discovered along the Northern and Southern borders. The North wanted control of it because they did not have arable lands and felt the people of the south had such lands and could do well enough as an agrarian community.

The media went as far as claiming oil as the root cause of civil war in Sudan. Oil is a secondary cause of dispute between rival Sudanese. Oil started being produced in Sudan in the late 1970s and has become the mainstay of the economies of the north and south.

OIL-BASED CONFLICT

In 1997, the government, now in possession of a larger number of oil fields throughout Sudan, needed to come up with a way to attract foreign oil industry investment to Sudan. To make oil investment more attractive, the government of Sudan began to draw up peace agreements. These agreements would establish peace between various political groups, especially in regions that contained the richest oil fields. While these agreements argued for peace in oil-heavy regions, peace was not achieved. The northern government armed various Nuer tribes with weapons and equipment and sent them off to fight other African tribes (Derks and Romer, 2008). When foreign investors would ask questions regarding conflict in the region, the northern government would respond that the conflict was the result of naturally occurring civil unrest between local tribes, a minor event of no concern to investors.

To make the situation worse, in addition to setting up internal conflict between tribes, the government did not adequately honor nor implement the peace agreements as written. Instead, the government of northern Sudan did the opposite, deploying additional forces in and around oil-rich regions. Two years later, in 1999, the first oil pipeline was completed and oil production could begin.

The profits earned by the northern Sudanese government from the sale of oil were used to reinvest in the military's efforts to take over South Sudan. This created even greater imbalance within Sudan. The individuals hardest hit by this increased imbalance were civilians in villages who lived near the oil fields. Thousands of civilians continued to be killed, taken into slavery, and displaced as their homes were looted and destroyed.

The conflict in Sudan over oil and other issues has resulted in the death of hundreds of thousands of individuals and the displacement of millions of Sudanese, including myself. The conflict around oil is deeply tied into the country's current macroeconomic situation. Oil is Sudan's leading export, accounting for 92 percent of all exports from Sudan. With Sudan in a state of post-conflict, the country as a whole currently stands in a better position than a lot of other postwar nations. Sudan, although better off than other regions of the world that are in a state of post-conflict, has a gross domestic product that is approximately fifty percent of the average African state (Derks and Romer).

Although oil is the greatest contributor to the Sudanese economy, it employs a relatively small percentage of the Sudanese workforce. Only four percent of the population contributes directly to the production of oil. Another eight percent of the labor force in Sudan participates in oil's supportive industries. This eight percent performs construction and infrastructure work such as building pipelines, refineries, roads, power stations, and dams. Although the United States, parts of Europe, and the United Nations have imposed economic sanctions and embargoes on Sudan, in an attempt to protect and deter the violence and the many injustices caused by the northern Sudanese government during the second Sudanese civil war, these actions taken on behalf of Asian industries and governments have negated the positive impact by western governments to help deter and stop the humanitarian injustices that have occurred in South Sudan.

CLEARING THE SOUTH

Beginning in 1983, President Nimeiri began to equip and train northern soldiers for an invasion of southern Sudan. The Dinka and Nuer tribes held large sections of land that had vast petroleum potential. In addition to the approach of northern soldiers to clear the land for oil, Nimeiri began to recruit members of the Nuer tribe to help with the process. Once the soldiers were in place, they would attack villages, driving out the residents, displacing them, and leaving the land clear for northern officials to move in and begin drilling for oil. Attacks such as these forced this author – along with many others – to march across Sudan into safety in Ethiopia, creating a vast diaspora.

Again, Abel Derks and Eugenie Romer stated that by 1986, the government's forces, invading from the north, acquired possession of most of the western upper Nile River. This is a unique case of "intra-national" invasion, where a portion – whether minority or majority – of a country would invade internally. At this point, the government was holding talks regarding a possible peaceful settlement that would end existing bloodshed and prevent it in the future. However, one day before legislation would have been passed to suspend Sharia law, a political revolt occurred, led by an Arabic organization called the National Islamic Front.

The National Islamic Front was led by northern general Omar al-Bashir, the future president of Sudan. This revolt, rather than suspending Sharia law and encouraging steps toward peace within Sudan, resulted in an increased persecution of individuals, an even louder call for the north to wage jihad upon the south, the eventual occupation of Osama bin-Laden during the 1990's, and the advent of a band of non-Arabic, non-Islamic political parties operating within the Sudanese government.

After incensed relations for an extended period, war soon broke out in what became the first Sudanese civil war in 1955-1972, in which some 100,000 combatants died and some 400,000 civilians also lost their lives. It was resolved in the Addis Ababa agreement, which resulted in the establishment of the Southern Sudan Autonomous Region with various powers. This was only the façade of a resolution and the war soon continued in what is now known as the Second Sudanese civil war that lasted even longer. The war lasted from 1983 to 2005 and there were as many as two million casualties of civilian denizen. It was resolved by the Comprehensive Peace agreement in which North Sudan signed a peace agreement. Additionally, there was the drawing up of the 2011 referendum and the South Sudan republic was established as an independent republic.

Although the war ended, the people were still reeling from the effects of it. A lot of Sudanese boys and girls were displaced after first enduring the harrowing experience of starvation, poverty, displacement, rape, and forced enlistment into barbaric child armies that did more evil to their psyche than good. They fled across many miles of desert lands into countries such as Ethiopia, Kenya, and other Diasporas. Collectively they constitute what is now known as The Lost Boys and Lost Girls of Sudan. Sadly enough, there is still influence of war in the Sudan as the deluded sect called the Lord's Resistance Army, under the leadership of Joseph Kony murder thousands.

When genocide was renewed in 1987 tens of thousands fled to Ethiopia on foot, some walking a thousand miles with next to no adult supervision. The youngest of the group was three and the oldest being teenagers, somewhat still kids themselves. Only 40,000 survived into Ethiopia. Four years later a military coup in that country forced them to flee back into Sudan and then south to Kenya. The six month ordeal saw their numbers reduced to 9,000, with most of them dying by bullets and bombs, attacks by crocodiles, or drowning in the rivers. They arrived in Kenya as walking skeletons.

They continued their education in camps in Ethiopia. In 2000, the U.S. government began resettling some of these boys and girls who were orphans. Today there are 4,500 Sudanese boys and girls located in the US, with several thousand in Australia and Canada.

Through all this ethnic and cultural war, Christianity has survived against all odds in this region and it is even becoming stronger, despite the age long persecution by the Muslim peoples. Most of the priests and deacons in Africa of this renewed Church are Lost Boys and Girls themselves. Many of the Lost Boys of Sudan are now Bishops and hold other similar leadership positions in the Christian church. It will be the focus of this book to portray the lives of a number of these boys and detail how Christianity, through the mysterious workings of the Lord, survived in this prophetic war ravished land.

INTRODUCTION

As a survivor of the atrocities committed by Sudanese forces, I feel compelled to shed light on the devastation that has been inflicted upon my home country.

I was born in a village in what is now South Sudan, but at age five I, along with many members of my family, was forced to flee my home due to the civil war raging between North and South Sudan. Alongside thousands of Sudanese refugees, I sought refuge first in Ethiopia, but upon the breakout of war there, we were forced to flee to a refugee camp in Kakuma, Kenya.

Forced out of my village at gunpoint, I trekked over 2,500 miles on barefoot. For eight years I lived in a refugee camp. There I learned I would be resettled in the United States. Because of this my life was changed forever.

I am a product of the United Nations High Commissioner for Refugees (UNHCR). I grew up in a UNHCR-run camp in Kakuma, Kenya and began formal education through a UNICEF-funded program.

At the age of fifteen, I was resettled in Grand Rapids, Michigan and placed in the care of a foster family. My experience mirrored that of the other 3,800 Sudanese children who were resettled in various parts of the United States. In recent times, by contemporary reckoning, 'The Lost Boys and Girls of Sudan' are the closest that many Americans have come to the tragedy of the Sudan. This is the general name given to a group of people who suffered by running the harrowing gauntlet of displacement from their lands and their homes. Most, if not all of them, were orphaned and fled their country with nothing but their lives.

In 1987, in America, while Michael Jackson was releasing his third album and Microsoft was introducing Windows 2.0, genocide was renewed in Sudan. Tens of thousands fled to Ethiopia on foot; some walking a thousand miles with next to no adult supervision.

The People's Armed Forces were given orders to "guard the oil... and work for evacuation of all other forces from the routes leading to oil exploration and roads. Also they were ordered to relocate all civilians to inside towns" (Talisman Court). While my people were being massacred, oil companies with investments in these tribal lands stood back and did nothing to prevent the murder of civilians. Rather than taking steps to end the suffering, the oil companies began to request security from the People's Armed Forces. In some instances they even assisted the army by providing logistical support to their military offensives (Derks and Romer).

In the early 1980's, seventeen thousand boys fled their homeland without their parents. The civil war in Sudan was turning their villages into burning heaps, killing the men and sending women and children fleeing for their lives. If the boys remained, they would have been recruited into the army of the Northern Muslims or killed. The boys chose the dangerous alternative of walking across Sudan to Ethiopia. Many boys lost their lives on the journey.

After walking for three months across Sudan they arrived at a refugee camp in Ethiopia. Twelve thousand boys made it to the camp where they lived for four years. When civil war broke out in Ethiopia they were forced at gunpoint to flee once more. They were chased to the Gilo River and forced into the water. Those who could not swim drowned or were killed by crocodiles and hippos. More than two thousand boys died trying to cross the Gilo River. Some were shot as they attempted to flee. Bodies of the dead floated down the Gilo.

They once more began to walk across the desert in Sudan. Of the original forty thousand, only ten thousand boys made it to the refugee camp in Kenya. There they lived for many years on little food and a lot of hope. By the fall of 2000, hope faded as the war continued and the idea of repatriation seemed futile. The United States government agreed to bring 4,000 of the Lost Boys to the US for resettlement.

The International Rescue Committee assisted in these efforts and helped resettle these boys, turned men into the largest cities in the country. Atlanta, Boston, Dallas, Phoenix, Salt Lake City, San Diego, Seattle. Tucson and Washington DC became home to the Lost Boys of Sudan. Assistance consisted of a few months' rent, job assistance and the barest of basic living necessities. They were left much of the time to fend for themselves and figure out how to survive in this new world.

The term refugee is understood in broad terms to mean persons fleeing war, civil strife, famine and/or environmental disaster. The concepts of exile, asylum, refuge, sanctuary and migration are old as man himself. International law protects refugees through the United Nations High Commissioner of Refugees. Many organizations help refugees from small private charities to large international institutions, some are faith-based and others are governmental organizations. One African proverb says it takes a village to raise a child. In this case it takes thousands of people to save refugees.

Both Sudanese and South Sudanese refugees have a different geo-political and economic rationale for leaving their country, which contrasts reports presented by the national and international media. Both national and international media have been reporting extensively on the curse of oil in the Sudan, but failed to report on basic humanity violations and the root cause of civil war, which have taken the lives of over two million people.

Not only have these oil industries, with massive business interest in the nation, promoted the country's destruction, but the corrupt government – the people who have turned against their country – has wreaked havoc as well. As 1 Timothy 6:10 states, "for the love of money is the root of all evil." These countries, in their greed for money, have brought great evil upon Sudan.

This book asserts the understanding of the root cause of the civil wars in Sudan, which will be essential to formulate the long waited reasons for partition and the future foreign relations between the two nations and beyond. The book is based on my personal experience, and on research and interviews conducted over the course of two years. The research involved those displaced by wars in Sudan and in particular, those who cannot return to their place of birth.

This book discusses the ethnological characteristics of the people who lived in various parts of Sudan who, as a result of war, have cemented their communities with their blood. In this writing, I've attempted to trace the historical evidence of animosity and the degree of political, cultural, and economic cohesion.

The process of writing the book will invite regional and international dialogue and reflection among any Sudanese whose faith is rooted in the joyous cry, "God did not abandon us!" In fact, there will come a time when the Lord will gather us among his scattered peoples and we will be with Him.

As the Sudanese have sacrificed to God, literally in the giving of their lives, God has, in turn, manifested himself among the Sudanese in a way that is beyond reason. The Lord, after all, works in mysterious ways, and it is not for man to question these ways, but instead to pray about them that they may be revealed. As far as these revelations are concerned, the Lord sends his prophets to guide us and warn us. This book will also look at the prophets in Sudan who have proclaimed his Word.

In an age where the American society prospers beyond the imagination of any previous generations, and generally more exceedingly so than most (if not all) other societies of the world today, the vitality of the devastated and persecuted Church of the Sudan stands equally beyond comprehension; In and through their suffering and the death of their martyred members.

CHAPTER 1:

THE LAND OF CUSH

*In history's annals the appearance of truth lies
awaiting the latter years to soothe the deep
yearning of his curiosity to know what has been
and what may yet be.*

Le Corbeau

The people of the Sudan have a very rich background
with a proud heritage. The ravaging sickle of war was no
stranger to them. The Cush, the former name of one of the
oldest tribes in the world, were very active in conquests the
world over. Many of Sudanese decent may not know (partly
because their name has over time evolved to be called the
Nubian kingdom,) that their great ancestor was Cush, the
oldest son of Ham and a much older brother to Canaan.

The Bible traces the genealogy from the great deluge to
the descendants of Cush. One important factor to also note
about how places are named is the principle or axiom
regarding the names of the peoples and nations listed in
Genesis ten and in other parts of the Old Testament. English
readers and scholars of the Bible have a great tendency to tie
the names to a fixed locality: we look upon them as
essentially "PLACE-NAMES." This was not the case with the

Hebrew readers in whose tongue the Bible or most of the Bible was originally written. To the Hebrews, these names are next after the individual who originally bore them, family-names for the descendants.

They, thus, stand for family groups, tribes, and nationalities. The names are essentially "RACE-NAMES." Wherever the race goes the name goes with them. The names are attached to the people rather than the place. So, for example, the Israelites once inhabited Goshen in Egypt; this did not make Goshen become Israel, but the people made Israel, so when they engaged in the great exodus, it was all of Israel comprising of the Israelites, that was migrating, not Goshen.

According to the book of Chronicles, of the children of Israel; "The sons of Ham; Cush, and Mizraim, Put, and Canaan. And the sons of Cush; Seba, and Havilah, and Sabta, and Raamah, and Sabtecha. And the sons of Raamah; Sheba, and Dedan. And Cush begat Nimrod: he began to be mighty upon the earth." This already establishes the strength of the people of Sudan, and also, the prophet Isaiah talked about the people of Israel.

It has been discovered that the Greek, three centuries before Christ came, when translating the Old Testament (which was at this time nothing but scrolls) from Hebrew, had employed the vague term Ethiopia as a replacement for the Hebrew word Cush. This is where the confusion originated. The meaning is that virtually all the representations of any Ethiopian individual in the Bible area mistranslation that should actually mean a Cushite.

These Cushites were originally descended from Cush, the son of Ham, the son of Noah, the latter of which were part of the renowned eight, having survived the great deluge. As recorded in Biblical text, Ham was cursed by his grandfather, Noah, after beholding Noah's drunken nakedness. It was also

28

clear, that according to the genealogies of the sons of Noah that the descendants of Cush were great people of the Lord. As can be found in Genesis 10:8-9, Cush was also the father of Nimrod who grew to be a mighty warrior on the Earth; "Cush was also the ancestor of Nimrod, who was the first heroic warrior on earth." Since he was the greatest hunter in the world, his name became proverbial. People would say, "This man is like Nimrod, the greatest hunter in the world."

With such powerful ancestry, it is not difficult to use the basic principles of genetics to know what race is being talked about in the book of Isaiah 18: "Go, swift messengers! Take a message to a tall, smooth-skinned people, who are feared far and wide for their conquests and destruction, and whose land is divided by rivers."

The Sudanese are a tall people, a smooth skinned people, with a violent history. There was a time when the Cushites conquered Egypt – which had been the superpower of its day. To the Egyptians, Sudan was known as the land of Cush – the source of ivory, incense, ebony, gold and slaves. Sudan was subjected to numerous Egyptian trading and raiding forays until the 8th century B.C. Then Cush grew to be a great power and, under their king Piankhi, the Cushites conquered Egypt in 712 B.C. The Assyrians later invaded and seized Egypt from Cushite control in 671 B.C.

The prophecy in Isaiah 18 could well refer to Southern Sudan. It speaks of a land "beyond the rivers of Ethiopia" which worships the Lord God. The prophecy declares that there will be great bloodshed there and a spiritual revival. Many people believe it accurately describes Southern Sudan today. In Zephaniah 3:10, a similar prophecy is given: "My scattered people who live beyond the rivers of Ethiopia will come to present their offerings."

From the beginning of the rich history of the Cushites, the people have unfailingly submitted themselves to God, letting his will be done, and fiercely defending the affairs of the Lord. In fact, for those who think that only the Israelites are the people of the Lord God, they had best peruse their Bibles even more closely. The Lord mentioned the Cushites among the forgotten and scattered ones he will gather as the remnants of his people from certain nations of the world. According to Isaiah 11:11; "In that day the Lord will reach out his hand a second time to bring back the remnant of his people – those who remain in from Assyria, and from Egypt, and from Pathros, and from Cush, and from Elam, and from Shinar, and from Hamath, and from the islands of the sea" (emphasis mine).

In recent years Christians and Jews who dwelt in this part of the Sudan were dispelled into South Sudan, and further into Eastern Africa. Some of them reached as far as the horn of Africa. The descendants of Cush have spread all over the world due to fifty years of suffering in war fare – war over identities, religion, and political ideologies. However, they have maintained their faith and their religion, as well as their traditions, beliefs, and cultural heritage and values, by forming communities and bringing up their children in the same way they would have done had they remained in their lands where they had been dispelled from.

This, perhaps, can again bring us to the story of Moses in the Bible who took an Ethiopian woman to be his wife, much to the displeasure of both his siblings; Aaron and Mariam. According to the book of Numbers, "Miriam and Aaron criticized Moses because he had married a Cushite woman. They said, "Has the Lord spoken only through Moses? Hasn't he spoken through us, too?" But the Lord heard them (Now Moses was very humble – more humble than any other person on earth.)So immediately the Lord called to Moses, Aaron, and Miriam and said, "Go out to the Tabernacle, all three of you!" So, the three of them went to the Tabernacle.

Then the Lord descended in the pillar of cloud and stood at the entrance of the Tabernacle. "Aaron and Miriam!" he called, and they stepped forward. And the Lord said to them, "Now listen to what I say: "If there were prophets among you, I, the Lord, would reveal myself in visions. I would speak to them in dreams. But not with my servant Moses. Of all my house, he is the one I trust. I speak to him face to face, clearly, and not in riddles! He sees the Lord as he is. So why were you not afraid to criticize my servant Moses?" The Lord was very angry with them, and he departed. As the cloud moved from above the Tabernacle, there stood Miriam, her skin as white as snow, free from leprosy."

Even though his own people were furious with him for taking an Ethiopian woman for a wife, the Lord showed he was not furious at this, but instead was furious at those who had questioned the activities of Moses. It means also that the Lord had very likely shown it unto Moses, or perhaps discussed it with him, that he had to take the Ethiopian woman for a wife even though the Lord had instructed the Israelites not to marry into other tribes. The Lord, therefore, was not disapproving of the Cushites. They were partly his people and that is why he could allow Moses, who was one of his most foremost prophets throughout the course of Israelite or Jewish history, to marry an Ethiopian woman.

The Cushites have always been a Prophetic race. This is not so just by the virtue of their being able to see things or dream dreams (in that regard, they very well may not be much different from any other race), but by the numerous things that have been said concerning them right from Biblical times. First, in the book of Joel 2:28, the Lord made a general prophecy through the Prophet Joel that said; "Then, after doing all those things, I will pour out my Spirit upon all people. Your sons and daughters will prophesy. Your old men will dream dreams, and your young men will see visions." The implication of this is that apparently, for every tribe, there will come a time when their young ones will become prophets, and they will prophesy. The people of Sudan, having faced much persecution, trials and tribulation at the hand of invading Arabic Muslims, and at their own hands in some instances, have begun to witness the fulfillment of this prophecy in their own lands.

Did the book of Psalms in the Bible not prophecy that; "Princes shall come out of Egypt; Ethiopia shall soon stretch out her hands unto God?" By Ethiopia, of course, the tribe or race being referred to is not the Ethiopia of today. The people being referred to here are the Cushites who later became the Nubian people and who are today, in the geographical region, called the Sudan. (Of course, this nomenclatural dynamism was brought about by the Arabization that swept into Africa from the North and North-East. This prophecy soon came to pass for it was quite a while afterwards that the marauding Sennacherib of Assyria began to express his colonial interest in Israel by way of siege, and baleful missives. It was then that the courageous King Tirhakah, King of the Cushites, sent forth an army to help the people of Israel by confronting Sennacherib. This is one of the true manifestations of Ethiopia stretching out her hands unto God.)

Another point to note is the Cushites have very receptively accepted the gospel of the Lord. The book of Acts 8 narrates to us Phillip's encounter with an 'Ethiopian' Eunuch, which of course meant with a Cushite Eunuch.

"As for Philip, an angel of the Lord said to him, "Go south down the desert road that runs from Jerusalem to Gaza."So he started out, and he met the treasurer of Ethiopia, a eunuch of great authority under the Kandake, the queen of Ethiopia. The eunuch had gone to Jerusalem to worship, and he was now returning. Seated in his carriage, he was reading aloud from the book of the prophet Isaiah. The Holy Spirit said to Philip, "Go over and walk along beside the carriage." Philip ran over and heard the man reading from the prophet Isaiah. Philip asked, "Do you understand what you are reading?" The man replied, "How can I, unless someone instructs me?" And he urged Philip to come up into the carriage and sit with him. The passage of Scripture he had been reading was this:

"He was led like a sheep to the slaughter. And as a lamb is silent before the shearers, he did not open his mouth. He was humiliated and received no justice. Who can speak of his descendants? For his life was taken from the earth." The eunuch asked Philip, "Tell me, was the prophet talking about himself or someone else?" So beginning with this same Scripture, Philip told him the Good News about Jesus. As they rode along, they came to some water, and the eunuch said, "Look! There's some water! Why can't I be baptized?" He ordered the carriage to stop, and they went down into the water, and Philip baptized him. When they came up out of the water, the Spirit of the Lord snatched Philip away. The eunuch never saw him again, but went on his way rejoicing."

This perhaps was the original reception of Christianity in the land of Cush. We, therefore, find that the Lord has always maintained a close relationship with the people of Cush and so, without doubt, the prophecy about the young people prophesying and the old men dreaming dreams could very well relate to them. Again, we are not surprised to find that in these times of war, the Lord, in his infinite mercies, has lifted up people and ordained them prophets in the Sudan to guide the bishops, the Church, the commanders in the direction God wanted them to go. The question now is who were these young people whom the Lord chose as prophets? What were their lives like? And who were they, those who died?

CHAPTER 2:

MY JOURNEY

*Tis in me now – the power, the courage
to dine with the devil with my bare hands
and cheat him for all his cunning, his age
till he no more wanders my glorious lands*

Le Corbeau

The Faith of Father Madhil

When Father Madhil woke up at 5.00 a.m. to say his morning prayers he did not know, despite the fact that he had been expecting it for a long time, that today it was his turn to have a stare down with the devil and his most menacing minion: Death. Father Madhil lived in the Nuba Mountains, not because he was born there but because that was where the Spirit had led him to minister. Originally, he hailed from Abyei in South Sudan, growing up there with his parents.

Father Madhil was an orphan who lost both parents to the first Sudanese war when he was about twelve years old. His elder brother had died the week before and was still being mourned when disaster came calling on the village. The ravagers arrived en masse, some thirty beastly men, disrupting the peace in the wee hours of the morning. They dragged people out of their houses and raped the women with lecherous glee. They derived joy from taking turns on the pregnant women.

Then, they lined up all the adults side-by-side on their knees, with hands behind their bowed heads. Facing them, were the children of the village and behind them glowed the incendiary horror of what used to be their houses and property. The inferno in the background lent a fiery glint to the marauders' eyes. Even the livestock had not been spared from carnage, for they too were slaughtered. As the children looked on, the attackers emptied the magazines of their guns into the bodies of the parents and promised the children a similar fate if they refused to comply with their commands.

It was then that young Madhil, who was an epileptic, was seized with a convulsive fit. While he lay writhing helplessly on the ground, the attackers abandoned him. But the deed had been done; he had witnessed the execution of his parents, and from that day forward he was also separated from his younger brother.

Homeless and helpless, Madhil wandered the land. Finally, he made his way to the town of Radom in Southern Darfur, where he was taken in by a white missionary, Father Francis. Madhil was raised in this setting and was instructed in the Christian faith as a young lad. He also acquired a western education and became well-grounded in the ways of the Lord. It was also here, when he was in his late twenties, that Madhil received his calling into the service of the Most High and proceeded to spread the gospel to the indigenous people who make their homes in the Nuba Mountains. At first, he tried to escape this calling, because he could not fathom the idea of going to dwell in the remote corners of the earth.

He was also wary of the underdevelopment of the region. At that time it had no electricity and no decent water supply.

Nonetheless, Madhil went out and ministered successfully in the region. He was able to clear some land for the multiple purposes of worshipping the Lord and schooling the little children.

One fateful morning, as he awoke to pray, the Spirit prompted him to read from the book of Jeremiah 1:5. He rose, picked up his Bible, navigated to the book of Jeremiah, and read, "I knew you before I formed you in your mother's womb. Before you were born I set you apart and appointed you as my prophet to the nations."

He wondered why this specific verse had been given to minister to him. Usually, this verse was used to convince new prophets to begin the work of the Lord. However, Madhil felt he was already a veteran in the Lord's work and had no need for the verse in question. Then he heard the first explosion.

He could not even identify with certainty the exact sound. All he heard was a great whistling whoosh and then a boom. It came from the west of the Nuba Hills. The first one came as a bit of a shock, and for the first five seconds that followed, there was an uneasy silence everywhere. Then, on the sixth second, the second whoosh-bang occurred and a motley variety of cries, wails, shrieks. Father Madhil ran out of his hut reciting Hail Marys as fast as he could. He saw everyone running pell-mell to the east, toward a small stream. He hurried along with everyone else, a more incessant series of whoosh-bangs propelling them on their way. That was when they discovered the ambush. Islamic fundamentalists from the North, many of whom were South Sudanese rebels, had used the aerial volley to push the villagers from one end of the hills to the next. All the while, the armed rebels lay in wait for them.

More significantly, the area they chose for the grand ambush was the very clearing Father Madhil had made and now used as a church and a school for the Muslim children of the mountains. This was not the first time the village had been attacked. There had been previous attacks before Father Madhil moved to the village. In this attack, the villagers, despite their Muslim faith, were still persecuted, tortured, and raped because of their ethnicity. At that time they had come to the realization that religion was just a façade the fundamentalist Cushites used to persecute the South Sudanese population. It was, therefore, a blessing that shortly thereafter, Father Madhil came along with love as the central theme of his gospel message. The people embraced the religion wholeheartedly and Father Madhil had even been able to conscript the services of two more pastors from his old mentor, Father Francis.

On this morning that promised great doom, the rebel soldiers were lying in wait on the grounds of what would have been Father Madhil's church. They quickly sprang up, brandishing an arsenal rich enough to sustain the genocidal intent of their hearts. They lined up all the villagers, patiently separating the women and children, then began to execute the men. They had proper intelligence regarding when and where to go in the village. They also knew the village contained a promising population of Christians.

The male children were going to be castrated, they said, and conscripted into the rebel army. Two of them began to lead the children away. The female children and their mothers would be used as either sex slaves or for menial jobs in their camps. Father Madhil and all the other men were forced to kneel down shamefully. He found himself in the same posture as his parents just before *they* were executed. He decided he was not going to die in the same manner. Instead of lifting his hands behind his head as he was ordered, he genuflected, and started to recite the Apostles' Creed while simultaneously, praying to God. He closed his eyes and asked God to let him go in a blaze of glory if it really was his time to die.

As he was praying, he faintly heard the men questioning each man. Seeing as they spoke the native Nuer language, they had even come along with an interpreter for those who could not understand what they were saying. Generally the sessions went something like;

"Are you Christian or Muslim?"

The man would reply "Christian" and would be compelled to "denounce Christ and say Allah is the one true God." He would refuse, and his head would be hacked off clean from the shoulders with a battle axe. If the man agreed or if he was Muslim from the onset, he was made to stand aside while the others were dispatched to the world beyond.

Father Madhil had already heard one of the pastors denounce Christ and he had heard the head of the other pastor fall with a thud on the ground. He was at this stage, reciting some verses from the Apostle Paul's second letter to Timothy; "As for me, my life has already been poured out as an offering to God. The time of my death is near. I have fought the good fight, I have finished the race, and I have remained faithful. And now the prize awaits me – the crown of righteousness which the Lord, the righteous Judge, will give me on the day of his return. And the prize is not just for me but for all who eagerly look forward to his appearing."

They soon decapitated the man next to him, and when they reached Father Madhil, and questioned him, he did not even open his eyes to answer them. Instead, like Saint Stephen, he spoke saying, "Father, forgive them for they know not what they do." Then he started singing, "I'm coming home, I'm coming home, I'm coming home..." So it was that with pride and dignity, his mood stout, his faith strong, and his spirit unwavering that he dared hell to do its ignominious worst. The villain swung the axe and his head fell but his body continued genuflecting and giving glory to the Lord.

I watched in horror as all this happened.

I was Father Madhil's personal assistant and was training under him to be a priest. I was in the room with him when he woke to say his morning prayers; I was kneeling right next to him when his head fell. I saw the marauders' spirits fail them upon the death of Father Madhil. They let everyone go after he was killed. They turned, went back down the mountains and drove off. It was the miracle revealing the power and glory of God as reflected in the death of Father Madhil that finally repelled the attack.

The rebels left and never came back. Neighboring villages fled to the refugee camp at Yida, but I remained to continue the work Father Madhil started. My courage was renewed after witnessing the power of God that day. I was granted the grace to stare down the devil and death, and I vowed that till my dying day, I would serve the Lord. Only two of the women ever made it back, and the unsavory stories they told about their experiences in the camps of the rebels heart wrenching. It depicted the basest form of inhumanity, the grossest evidences of man's inhumanity to his fellow man that could possibly be imagined.

At that time I decided to pray fervently to the Lord to know my calling; I would not proceed to start a ministry that was not really mine to begin. I prayed and fasted for a full week, and finally, the answer came to me. Now, many may think I was asleep and dreaming. I saw myself preaching. Perhaps, others would assume I saw myself preaching, as the disciple of Jesus Christ, Simon Peter, did on the day of Pentecost. This happened after the Spirit of God had descended upon him and the others in the upper chamber; they were speaking in other tongues, and about three thousand souls got converted.

Others may assume I had a more dramatic experience like the Prophet Moses did before the burning bush; they imagine a still small voice whispered in my ear what would be my final calling, and I was to proceed immediately without fear of favor from any man. Neither was I asleep and made to eat a burning scroll.

No, my calling came to me in a real life experience, in the spur of the moment. I had gone to a lonely place to pray. As I was returning home, I passed by a house where a woman had apparently just lost her husband for she was wailing disconsolately. I felt the Spirit nudging me to speak with her. As I approached the compound, I noticed that the men were gathered in a bunch at a corner of the house. Some had their arms folded across their chests while others held their hands behind them. They all looked very sad. At the same time, the women were engaged in the herculean feat of consoling their weeping comrade.

I walked over and politely asked the women consoling her to stand aside and grant me an audience. They looked at me with surprise, but heeded my request and stepped aside. I am quite convinced that I had more surprise in my eyes than they had in theirs. I was only a stranger after all, and here I was requesting access to their close family member. I reached the woman's side and found her sitting on the floor beside two covered bodies. Turning to one of the other women, I asked who had died and she replied that these were the bodies of the woman's husband and only son. Looking at the woman, I could almost feel the pain and loss she was experiencing. I knew instinctively that it was her only child. She looked very young; perhaps she was twenty-two or twenty-three years of age and she was only just starting life. Besides, there were no other children crying there beside her. As I reached the young widow's side, I laid my hand consolingly on her shoulder and she turned to look up at me.

Perhaps, because of the Spirit moving heavily in me, or by virtue of the fact that I was a stranger and she wanted to hear me out, the woman kept quiet and remained still, looking at me. My throat was dry. I really did not know what to say to her, but as I opened my mouth, words started coming out. I did not know where the words were coming from, but I know they were good words, because they held not only her attention, but the attention of everyone around us. In twenty minutes, even the men who were bunched together when I entered had been drawn to find out what held the women in such rapt attention.

I continued to talk and gradually I noticed that the crowd was beginning to multiply in number. People who stopped by to check on the grieving family would enter the compound and the word the Lord was using me to utter was holding them spell-bound. After three hours, there were about two hundred and fifty people gathered to hear the message I was preaching. It was incredible. I did not know how it happened. I had started out preaching a message about death, and was trying to make her understand that it was just a challenge, or a trial that she was facing in her life. She would be alright if she remained steadfast in God. I had to narrate the story of Job to her, and she was quite impressed especially when she heard the part about how God restored everything to Job sevenfold.

The people grew curious to know what kind of God this was. I asked if they had ever heard anything about Jesus Christ or the Lord God himself. I told them how it was God who created the world. I showed them the principles the Lord had laid down for his people and how love was greatest of all of them. I told them how important it was for each person to love his neighbor. I gave an altar call and was surprised, but not at all mystified, to find that about four hundred people wanted to give their lives to Christ. I led them through the prayer process and even conducted a proper Christian burial for the dead. The people said they wanted to hear more. I privately called aside the new owner of the house (who happened to be the immediate younger brother of the deceased husband) and asked if he would allow us to use his home for the next meeting. He was only too happy to allow this, so I conveyed the time and date for the next meeting to the people. They were pleased to hear this.

I got to my room and began to give glory to the Lord for revealing my calling unto me. So I was supposed to be preaching about love and tolerance and the general goodwill of the Lord as he says in the book of Jeremiah 29:11, "For I know the plans I have for you, says the LORD, they are plans for good, and not for disaster, to give you a future and a hope." I was very excited about this and I committed the work wholly into the Lord's hands. I knew there could be no worse fate for me than failing in this one task which the Lord had appointed me for, so I prayed for guidance and mercy, and most importantly of all, I prayed for wisdom to do what the Lord wanted of me – His will.

By the time we met the following Sunday, there were more than the initial four hundred waiting. Within five months, we were about three thousand. The Lord had blessed the family whose house we were using so much that they had since moved out of the house to another location. The building that used to be their home now serves as the church building, and I did not pay a single dime for it. In fact, based on many offerings and contributions, I am working on expanding our Church, the Love Foundation Church of Sudan, well beyond its current limits, out into the general country, and on to the world as a whole.

All these things would not have even been possible – not to mention thriving or enduring – if I had not witnessed the death of Father Madhil. He had inspired me greatly. Following the war, when both Sudans – Northern and Southern – were about to separate, there was a heightened tempo of Arabic persecution. I was jailed five times, even though it was usually a single- or couple of nights' affair, usually for the most absurd reasons and on the most incredulous charges ever raised. Still, the important point is that I had no fear all along, and still experience no fear.

This is the reality of the martyrs. Their presence surrounds every Sudanese who has lost family members. It embraces them. But the faith of the martyrs paradoxically is the very substance that feeds the Church.

CHAPTER 3:

A SHIELD OF FAITH

Of all damnedest sins a man may commit,
None the more damning than theft
from God is For, be not deceived, that
man will remit Either all he stole from
God or his peace.

Le Corbeau

When adversity comes, the best a man can do is to be ready to confront it at all times. The ability to confront these challenges does not lie in the might or in the brain, but in the spirit. The principles to arm ourselves in the spirit against these adversities reside in the Bible. And even after being armed, one must have a significant amount of faith, which will serve as the activator for the superpowers that the Lord has left at our disposal. Many do not know the power they wield, but if one would read the book of Ephesians 6:12-18, one would find the complete armor lying there in wait. It reads, "For we are not fighting against flesh-and-blood enemies, but against evil rulers and authorities of the unseen world, against mighty powers in this dark world, and against evil spirits in the heavenly places. Therefore, put on every piece of God's armor so you will be able to resist the enemy in the time of evil. Then after the battle you will still be standing firm. Stand your ground, putting on the belt of truth and the body armor of God's righteousness. For shoes, put on the peace that comes from the Good News so that you will be fully prepared. In addition to all of these, hold up the shield of faith to stop the fiery arrows of the devil. Put on salvation as your helmet, and take the sword of the Spirit, which is the word of God. Pray in the Spirit at all times and on every occasion. Stay alert and be persistent in your prayers for all believers everywhere."

Fortunately for my best friend, Bong, he was well armed when adversity came. Now fifty-seven-years old, he originally emigrated from the Sudan as a relatively young lad. I was horrified to hear all he had been through. This is his account of his journey:

The Tale of Bong

I was suddenly awakened from my sleep by my older brother, who came to tell me that father was calling me. The thing about being awakened from sleep is that one is sorely tempted to shoot daggers at the intruder with one's eyes, then command such a person with the croaky voice of a sleepy man never to interrupt anyone's sleep again, and fall back blissfully into Somnus' embrace. But that is all there is to it – mere naked temptation. Did not the Bible warn the listening ear to be watchful and vigilant? And did the same Bible not beseech one by the mercies of God, to present the body a living sacrifice, holy, acceptable unto God, *which is* one's reasonable service, and to not conform to this world: but be transformed by the renewing of one's mind that one may prove what *is* that good, and acceptable, and perfect, will of God? Was it not God's will to honor one's father and mother that one's days may be long? I, therefore, knew there was naught for it but to do what I knew my elder brother,

Deng would not do. I compelled my body to stand up and heed father's call, even though I had only started sleeping.

I groggily walked out and found everyone hurriedly packing up things and hustling the cattle to get ready to move. We had set up camp for herding our cattle at Majak, not too far away, but some twenty five kilometers east of Bor. My father was head of the cattle camp, and I could see him frowning with worry as he gave out directions for the packing up of camp.

"Papa," I said to him as I drew near, "we only just got here. Why are we leaving in a hurry already?"

"There is no time for answering questions," he replied me. "The rebels have reached Bor, and will be here anytime soon. Pack your things and join your brother in moving out the cattle."

That was when my eyes really cleared. I had heard rumors for a while that the rebels could come to Bor anytime because they were displeased with something their former commander had done, but I did not believe it now that it was happening. My thoughts raced to Mary, the girl I had met just two weeks before we left Bor. I remembered her laugh – very rich and heart-warming – and then her comely visage, and her luscious body. Only one conversation had passed between us, and I had made a mental note to continue with her when I returned from grazing the cattle with father, brother, and the other men. She was working at St. Andrews' Episcopal Church compound, the same church where my sister worked and it was where we met. I had gone to tell my sister one thing or another (I really can't remember), a message from Mother that sent me on this errand. When I arrived, my sister was talking to Mary, so I got the introduction that was to set off the sparks of that volatile thing called love. It was a burning ring of fire, love. It did not scorch me, but it warmed me, made me feel alive, and so when Mary asked me if I had accepted Jesus Christ as my personal Lord and savior, I would only be too happy I was not my brother, Deng who had repelled incorrigibly all of sister's teachings. I was quite grounded in Christianity and I pointed that out to her. Alas, now word just reached me that Bor was an inferno. My stomach sank to the lowest regions of my bowels and I felt a false urge to empty them.

We set off hurriedly, father and the rest of us. We could only pray that Uncle Chol, father's elder brother, whom we had left at home, was doing a fine job of protecting the ladies at home. The cattle, perhaps groggy, or perhaps oblivious to the impending doom refused to hasten along, and when they finally did decide to hasten along, it was into muddy terrain. Rain had fallen earlier in the evening, making the ground mushy. The cattle made the mush worse, and soon enough, they required strong pushes to get out of the quicksand to which they were demiurgic.

We had only been out for about thirty minutes when my younger brother, Poni, whom we had left at home with sister, mother, and Uncle Chol, caught up with us. He reached us panting, and the whole lot of us, shocked, rapidly questioned him. Of course, he did not answer; it was not because he had a desire to be insolent, but because he was panting heavily and crying at the same time, so he really did not have enough breath to speak coherent words and did not bother trying. Father solved that problem by first ordering us to be quiet, then handing Poni his water bottle to sip from. He then sternly told Poni to be a man and soon enough, Poni was quite miffed at the idea of weeping. He became calm enough to tell us that Bor had suffered an incredible attack and that the attackers were moving our way, so we had best abandon the cattle and hide, let them pass us, then we could backtrack to Bor and see what was left, if anything, of our property.

Apparently, he had run for about a day and a half, barely resting in order to reach us so quickly.

Father was quiet. He pondered the situation very carefully and after a while, he ordered us to abandon the cattle and hide. We ran westward, away from the cattle, for about 10 minutes. When we were well away, we found a cluster of hills and hid there. After about an hour, we started hearing voices and could make out men coming from behind us on the path. It was dark, so we could not see what they were wearing, but we saw (because of the flaming torches they carried) that upon sighting the cattle, they stopped. There were very many, maybe a hundred, maybe two hundred in numbers, I can't tell, but they seemed heavily armed. They approached the cattle and seemed to search for something. Not finding it, they pumped bullets into the cattle, some of which ran away, while the others dropped dead having being struck by the bullets.

We watched in horror as this carnage took place, and Poni, still being very faint of heart, soon began to whimper even though he was already seventeen. The sight was gory, anyone would have cried to see their livelihood pumped full of lead. The only reason I was calm was probably because I was reciting from the book of Psalms 91; "Those who live in the shelter of the Most High will find rest in the shadow of the Almighty. This I declare about the Lord: He alone is my refuge, my place of safety; he is my God, and I trust him. For he will rescue you from every trap and protect you from deadly disease; He will cover you with his feathers. He will shelter you with his wings. His faithful promises are your armor and protection. Do not be afraid of the terrors of the night, nor the arrow that flies in the day. Do not dread the disease that stalks in darkness, nor the disaster that strikes at midday. Though a thousand fall at your side, though ten thousand are dying around you, these evils will not touch you. Just open your eyes, and see how the wicked are punished. If you make the Lord your refuge, if you make the Most High your shelter, no evil will conquer you; no plague will come near your home. For he will order his angels to protect you wherever you go. They will hold you up with their hands so you won't even hurt your foot on a stone. You will trample upon lions and cobras; you will crush fierce lions and serpents under your feet! The Lord says, "I will rescue those who love me. I will protect those who trust in my name. When they call on me, I will answer; I will be with them in trouble. I will rescue and honor them. I will reward them with a long life and give them my salvation."

The book of Psalms was my favorite book in the Bible. No matter what mood I was trapped in, I would simply read from there, and before long, I was bound to find a chapter conveying me back to my normal state. At the moment though, I was conducting myself very fearlessly even though I was in a very uncomfortable situation where I had to choose between whimpering and purging myself of the sorrow I felt – like my brother – and looking on very painfully, as my father was now doing. What they were doing, it seems, was that they were pursuing the scorched earth policy started by the Arab zed Muslims to the north. The policy was ignominious and it had been deployed as such.

Ten minutes later, we were disappearing; we left the spot where they killed the cows, and were soon well out of sight. We decided to go back to Bor to see how things were. When we walked on for a day and a third of another day and finally, we began to see what should have been familiar spots on the edge of the town. Only, these landmarks had been reduced to ashes. For example, we could see Mr. Garang's farm, fully razed to the ground. That was his only source of income and one of the town's main sources of food. There was no way he could recover from that. As we moved forward, we became acquainted with the full extent of the raid. There were bodies scattered everywhere; some strewn by the roadside, some that looked like they had been piled together before they were killed. Some were stark naked – they probably had been raped.

Poni tried to throw up, but since his stomach was empty, he simply kept retching. I knew then that death was the ravaging spirit that madmen with weapons unleash whenever they chance upon a few helpless people. What could these civilians possibly have been guilty of to warrant such a massacre? They had started off calling themselves the SPLRA, claiming to fight for the rights of the people. Then they had a misunderstanding amongst themselves and formed a breakaway faction called the SPLRA-Nasir. Now it was the very people for whom they were supposed to be fighting, that they were fighting *against*. Alas, if the people were even capable of defending themselves, it would have been a bit of a fight, but the people were defenseless and helpless, so it was more appropriate to say it was carnage, a massacre. My town of Bor was now the office where death had taken up its activities. So far, the only living things we had seen were flies, vultures, and other scavenging creatures that were feasting away on the dead bodies of our friends. We were too weak, too dispirited and disheartened to chase them away. We just stood there, mouths gaping and trying in vain to come to terms with things.

We headed on, trying to hurry, but our legs were weak, not from exhaustion, but from the heaviness of our hearts. When we finally reached what should have been our house, we were quite shocked and hopeful, an odd duo of mixed feelings, because it had not been razed to the ground. Fortunately, we could not find any bodies of relatives strewn about as was common with the other houses.

That gave us more hope, but when we entered, we found mother and uncle Chol lying still and quite dead on the floor. Apparently, the invaders did not come to rob us. Nothing was really out of place except for where there appeared to have been a struggle. Uncle Chol must have been shot at close range, for there was a gory hole in the middle of his forehead. Mother, on the other hand, had been dispatched so handily, it seemed. I did not want to imagine the horrible things they had done to her. Father could not take it anymore; he broke down and started weeping. Poni, who had only been looking for the chance, started wailing uncontrollably too. The other men had gone home to check on their families, so I raced outside to the St. Andrew's Episcopal Church compound.

The place had been torched. The roof had fallen in and the insides had really been hit. They did intend to destroy this place. However, it was at the back of the church that I observed the real damage. The senior reverend had been burnt alive, it seemed. Perhaps he failed to denounce Christ. I heard they burned or buried them alive for failing to do that. The ladies, well, they seemed to have suffered much worse fates. They were naked, mostly, and it seemed they had been raped for there was a lot of caked blood on some of their skirts. Some were shot point blank. The fiends had ravaged the lives of people who dedicated themselves to good and to the service of God. I knew God would punish them for this grievous offense against man and against Himself.

I was forced to wonder if God was even God. Why did he not protect his own when they were going through the torture they faced before they were killed? I could see my Rose, she too had apparently been defiled and I could not even bring myself to look upon her nakedness. I could not even find a decent cloth to cover her with. The same had been the case with my sister. They had suffered in their final moments.

I was lost in grief when the Lord ministered to me from the book of Matthew 5; "Blessed *are* they which are persecuted for righteousness' sake: for theirs is the kingdom of heaven. Blessed are ye, when *men* shall revile you, and persecute *you,* and shall say all manner of evil against you falsely, for my sake. Rejoice, and be exceeding glad: for great *is* your reward in heaven: for so persecuted they the prophets which were before you." I knew these dear ones were in Heaven, where their reward had been kept safe. They were probably in Father Abraham's bosom looking at me and hoping my faith would not waiver. I did not disappoint them.

I headed out, away from the whole mess, away from the great persecution. Ten years have passed. I thank God my faith remained strong and today I am the head pastor over the congregation of the revitalized St. Andrew's Episcopal Church. Every year, we hold a remembrance service for those who lost their lives in the massacre. Even though the town was set back by the unspeakable carnage, our people keep on moving forward steadily in the Faith. The people of Sudan are exceedingly strong, particularly those South Sudanese who are still carrying on their regular activities after everything they have been through.

I wish I could tell you this was the end of our troubles, but it was not. There are many like us all around the world. Many of us within Sudan continue to face internal persecution.

The Reality of a War-Torn Country

Yet, while some are making manifest the good works of the Lord, there are those evil agents who seek to discourage the work of the Lord. Even in the old days, there were those who dedicated themselves to this evil endeavor.

A worse dimension to the conflicts that has little or nothing to do with Christianity or religion at all is that when oil was discovered in Sudan, and it was found that most of the oil fields are located in South Sudan, the Arab Sudanese attempted various strategies to expel the Black Sudanese from their homes to turn the region of South Sudan into a mine.

The government removed the subsidies on fuel, which prompted the people to protest en masse. The government responded to their peaceful protest with live ammunition. The Human Rights Watch released an official report stating the extent of the extrajudicial killings that were going on in Sudan at this time:

On September 25, 2013, Hazza Eldin Jafar Hassan, age eighteen, was shot dead during demonstrations near his house in Bahri, Khartoum North. His mother told Human Rights Watch he was shot in the head around 3.00 p.m. by security forces in beige uniforms riding in a white vehicle.A student who participated in the protest with Hazza told researchers he saw several land cruisers carrying security forces wearing camouflage uniforms, approaching the protesters:

"The first [vehicles] fired rubber bullets and tear gas on us and the last two [vehicles] fired live bullets. I was standing on the side of the street when I heard the gunshots. I fell on the ground and...after it stopped I looked up to see Hazaa lying on the ground motionless. I crawled to him and flipped him over only to find him soaked in blood. He was bleeding from a gunshot wound to his head. He was already dead."

Hazza's mother, in a statement posted on YouTube, said family and friends found his body and carried him away amid continued gunshots. "We were carrying the body and still in pain over his death, they were still firing bullets around and tear gas," she recalled.

According to witnesses, the same evening, as family members and friends gathered for Hazza's funeral in the Shambat neighborhood, Hazza's friend Bashir al Nur Hammed, age twenty, was shot in the leg and the head, and died on the spot. Though Human Rights Watch could not establish details of the shooting, witnesses said national security forces driving in white vehicles were responsible.

On September 27, dubbed "Martyr's Friday" by Sudanese political activists, demonstrations against the killing of protesters started after midday prayers. Dozens were believed to have been killed on that day, amongst them Dr. Salah al-Din Sanhouri, a twenty-eight-year old pharmacist, who was shot in the back during a protest. Sanhouri's death became a symbol of the crackdown and rallying cry for anti-government protesters during the protests and in the media.

On that same day, in Bahri, Khartoum North, national security officials shot and killed twenty-year-old Osama Mohammadein el Amin while attempting to disperse a large group of protesters marching toward the North Bahri courts complex. One witness recalled how, after police allowed a protest to continue, armed security forces waiting at the complex beat protesters with sticks and shot at the crowd.

"The national security officials armed with Kalashnikov rifles and wearing camouflage, riding in four-wheel Toyota Land Cruisers, blocked our way. They threw teargas at us and told us to disperse. They started to beat us with sticks. We turned back toward the courts and stayed on the main road. While we were there we heard a gunshot and I saw Osama who was standing in front of me in the middle of the road fall down. He was shot in the head above his left eyebrow. At that time, there were national security agents in plainclothes and police standing in front of the courts. I am not sure who exactly shot him, but the gunshot came from them."

The same day Dr. Samar Mirghani Abu-Naouf, a pharmacist, recorded on her phone the killing of a boy by police officers during protests in her neighborhood. "While I was filming, a boy was shot and fell dead right in front of me, around two meters away. I was in a state of shock. I started screaming and I continued filming. I had documented the entire killing of the boy. The officers then approached me and snatched my phone," she recalled. Shortly after this, officers detained and beat her.

A large proportion of reported killings occurred in poorer suburbs like Mayo and Haj Yousif. Among the confirmed killings were Abdullah Yousif Suliman, an eighty-seven-year-old merchant, wounded by gunshots died four days later; and nineteen-year-old Omar Khalil Ibrahim Khalil and fifteen-year-old Saleh Sadiq Osman Sadiq, both killed at the Haj Yousif bus station by gunshots to the head on September 25, 2013.

Armed security forces that were deployed to disperse protests opened fire with live ammunition on protesters, killing scores.

"No one was carrying anything in their hands apart from their school bags," a witness told Human Rights Watch. When the protesters reached the police station, uniformed police and community police in plainclothes began firing live ammunition toward the protesters, causing them to disperse.

A short while later, at around 10:30 a.m., one of them fired a round of live ammunition at the protesters and killed a seventeen-year-old high school student, Mohammed Ahmed al Tayeb. Witnesses identified the shooter as a member of the community police who owned a shop in the neighborhood that was subsequently looted. "After this incident the protesters got angrier and started to throw stones and set fire to tires, and the police responded with bullets," the witness recalled. Some of the security forces went to the roof of a building and fired at protesters, killing and injuring several more.

In a nearby area on the same day, police shot a twenty-nine-year-old painter during a protest. According to witnesses, a crowd of protesters moved toward the police station and police officers shot bullets into the air and tear gas to disperse them. One witness heard one of the police officers say "shoot the long hair," referring to Mosa'ab:

In Althowra, Salaheldin Daoud Mohammed Daoud, a 65-year old amputee who lost his right arm in a car accident in 1966, and advocated for the rights of persons with disabilities, was shot in the knee while doing an errand near his home. In his neighborhood national security officers were shooting at youths, who were throwing bricks and stones. After a lull in the shooting Daoud, left his home, but was then shot in the left knee, requiring amputation of his left leg. "I don't think they targeted me specifically, but they targeted the youth," he said.

The national security entered the neighborhood in vehicles and chased youths on foot. In Aborouf, on September 25, police fired live bullets at protesters who were peacefully marching toward the police station, according to a witness who spoke to Human Rights Watch. In addition to shootings, security forces also severely beat protestors to disperse or punish them, or while arresting them. In one example from Wad Medani on September 23, Rania Mamoun, a journalist, and her two siblings were arrested during protests, beaten, and detained by security forces for a night at a police station. In a public statement entitled, "A day in Hell: My Testimony from the Arrest," Mamoun writes:

"My brother was hit on the head. I was hit by a large number of soldiers who circled me like flies. The beating was intense and meant to hurt and abuse...They dragged me on the ground and called me all sorts of names then threatened me with gang rape...With the continued beatings I reached the stage where I did not feel pain with every new strike that followed."

Another man was badly beaten by armed national security officers when he tried to intervene in the brutal beating of a nineteen-year-old boy:

They were dragging [the boy] on the ground and beating him with sticks and their gun butts. I told myself I must do something to rescue this boy. I came closer and told them, 'Please if he did something wrong, take him to your office and investigate but what you are doing is inhuman.' Then one of the high-ranking officers replied, 'Who are you? Are you telling us what to do?' and ordered me to get inside their pickup truck. Then about six of them grabbed me by the hands and legs and threw me on the back of the truck, then started beating me with sticks and plastic pipes and some were [stomping] on me with their boots.

Yousif el-Mahdi, a political activist, told Human Rights Watch how on September 29 following the funeral for Salah Sanhouri, national security officers arrested and beat him up. "A group of four or five officers in khaki uniforms beat me with their batons then threw me into the back of one of their pick-up trucks. I was made to lay on my front along with a young man who had also been tracked down and beaten," he recalled.

During this time, authorities reported arresting 600 people, while human rights organizations reported over 800 arrests. Although many of the protesters were released within hours or days, often following summary trials resulting in punishment of lashing or fines, large numbers remained in detention for weeks and even months, many without charge or access to family or lawyer visits.

Of those who were legally charged in connection with crimes committed during the September demonstrations, several dozen remained in detention as of late March 2014, including journalist Ashraf Omar Khogli and four minors who face charges of burning a police station. Sudanese lawyers have called for the release of all remaining detainees held in connection with the protests, and an end to the property crimes' trials, which they describe as deeply flawed and in violation of the Child Act of 2010. Human Rights Watch has not independently monitored these cases.

Many others, including youth activists, political party members, journalists, and human rights defenders were arrested because of their perceived anti-government views and role in organizing the demonstrations and were never legally charged. Former detainees reported a common pattern of being arrested often at night from their homes, taken to the nearest police office and interrogated, then transferred to a detention facility in various locations around Sudan. They were held in locations across the country for periods ranging from a few days to weeks or months.

Many of the detainees who spoke to Human Rights Watch reported that they were beaten, verbally abused, and forced to hand over passwords to e-mail or Facebook accounts, and were released only after signing a promise not to participate in protests or other actions against the state. The treatment appeared worse for Darfuris, especially student members of the United Popular Front, a Darfuri student group linked to the Sudan Liberation Army faction led by Abdel Wahid al-Nur. Some told Human Rights Watch that they had been, or had seen others, who were subjected to electrical shocks.

Sudan's police force, NISS, operates dozens of official and unofficial detention facilities in Khartoum and Omdurman alone, some in office buildings and others in residential compounds. Many detainees were held at the NISS political headquarters in Bahri. The facility consists of several buildings, including one known as "Guantanamo," due to its extreme temperatures, bright lights and reputation for use of torture tactics against detainees held there.

While treatment in detention varied, depending on the political and social profile of the detainee, in all cases, detainees reported experiencing some form of verbal abuse such as racist and sexist slurs.

It is needless to warn the government officials of Sudan that their actions will be held against them if they do not cease all the inhumanity it is currently basking in. In order to protect its own interest, the government keeps making unconstitutional attacks. The people are displaced, starved, and hungry, but that still does not mean the attacks will stop. In fact, sadly, that seems to be the point and aim of all the attacks that are being leveled against South Sudan – a series of planned and strategically executed operations to clear certain areas in South Sudan, so that the government can troop in to start drilling oil for free without having to answer to any party aside from itself. This level of sadism is appalling to hear in the 21st century, seeing as there are now global bodies monitoring this kind of conduct, but then, the people of Sudan have always been terrible from their beginning and given to wars and violence. Despite a façade that seems to show that they are moving with the times, as far as diplomacy and human relations are concerned, there seems to be no real development in the government's management of its internal affairs, and this is constantly recurring.

More tragic suffering was inflicted in the civilians of Sudan when a mass rape occurred in Darfur. The Human Rights Watch released a forty eight page report, detailing how Sudanese army troops went from house to house in the

North Darfur town of Tabit last October and raped over 221 civilian girls and women in just a 36-hour time span. According to the report, "Over the course of 36 hours beginning on October 30, 2014, Sudanese army troops carried out a series of attacks against the civilian population of the town of Tabit in North Darfur, Sudan. The attacks included the mass rape of women and girls and the arbitrary detention, beating and ill-treatment of scores of people. The government of Sudan has denied that any crimes occurred and has prevented the African Union-United Nations Hybrid Operation in Darfur (UNAMID) from carrying out a credible investigation of the incident.

Sudanese government forces carried out the rapes and other abuses during three distinct military operations against the town during the 36-hour period: the first beginning the evening of Thursday, October 30 2014 until the second morning, November 1. Human Rights Watch found no evidence of a presence of any rebel force in the town immediately prior to or during the attacks.

Witnesses told Human Rights Watch that during each of these attacks, government soldiers went house-to-house in Tabit, searching houses, looting property, severely beating residents, and raping women and girls. On the two nights, soldiers forced many of the men to outdoor locations on the outskirts of the town, leaving the women and children especially vulnerable. The soldiers detained the men en masse, and threatened and physically abused them throughout the night.

Residents recognized some of the soldiers as among those stationed at the Sudanese Armed Forces (SAF) base on the outskirts of the town. The aims of the military operations against Tabit are unclear. Numerous residents told Human Rights Watch that government soldiers entering their homes said that they were looking for a soldier who had been abducted and to punish his captors. One soldier who later defected told Human Rights Watch that they had been ordered to search for and punish rebel supporters in the town because of information that rebel forces deployed outside the town were planning to attack the SAF base. Two soldiers who had participated in the operations said that superior officers had ordered them to "rape women" because the women were rebel supporters.

Most of the rape victims interviewed by Human Rights Watch said they were unable or unwilling to be treated at Tabit's limited medical facilities because they feared arrest and further physical abuse by government officials.

The exact number of women and girls who were raped or subjected to sexual violence by Sudanese military personnel in Tabit will not be known until independent and impartial investigators with expertise in sexual and gender-based crimes are granted unfettered access to Tabit and town residents feel safe to share their experiences without fear of retaliation.

They were able to conduct some phone interviews to determine exactly what happened there. These are some of the accounts of the women who were raped.

Human Rights Watch interviewed fifteen women who said they were raped by soldiers. Most said they were raped multiple times, often by multiple men, and often in front of their families or friends. Almost all reported that they were also severely beaten.

Mahassan, in her twenties, said that she and three friends were raped by soldiers after sunset. They were in her home preparing perfumes for a wedding when about ten soldiers entered the compound, dragged the women outside, and raped each of them multiple times:

"[The soldiers] said that they were looking for a missing soldier. They searched the compound. [Then] they came towards us. They grabbed me and they grabbed my friends. The other soldiers took the other girls in a different direction. They took [me and my friend outside of the compound] towards the school. They raped both of us on the street. ... Three of them raped me and three of them raped my friend. ... They raped us all night. That's why I'm still sick. I cannot sit down for a long time like I could before."

Around the same time, another woman, Maria, in her forties, encountered soldiers blocking the road to town as she was returning from her farm. She said:

I wanted to pass. They stopped me. I refused to stop and one cocked his gun. He said that if I didn't stop he would shoot me. I asked why. He said, "Your men killed our guy." I was on a donkey. Then he pulled me [off the donkey]. Then three other [soldiers] came. They surrounded me. Then they beat me. They raped me. Then they went and left me.

She said two of her neighbors were also raped that evening.

Around the same time, another woman, Umm-Jumma, in her thirties, heard screaming and fled with her children to her mother's compound, where soldiers arrived and asked her if she was hiding a missing soldier, then beat and tied up her mother. Umm-Jumma described how she attempted to resist them:

I fought one and hurt one. When they saw that I wanted to fight they threatened me with their gun. Then they raped me. There were four of them. Two had civilian clothes. [They raped me] in front of my mother. She was screaming.

After they left she recalled hearing gunshots and the sound of women screaming from other compounds. She also realized that her child, who was snatched from her by a soldier and thrown against the wall, had broken his leg and arm.

Khamisa, in her twenties, said she was beaten and then raped by soldiers and men in civilian clothes at the gate of her neighbor's compound:

I found a soldier at the gate of my neighbor's house. The soldier stopped me. When he stopped me I hit him with a stick on the head. Then he hit me with the butt of his gun. When he hit me, I fell down. Before I realized anything there were two men holding me down [and raping me].

She said she recognized two of the three men who raped her as residents of Tabit. She saw both of them in the market the following day.

Jameya, in her late twenties, was in her compound with her husband, cooking dinner, when several soldiers arrived. She said:

"[The soldiers] said that they were looking for a missing solider. They searched and found nothing. They asked me to get up and they said, "Don't cook that food." I refused to get up. Then one of them hit me with the butt of his gun. I fell down. My head was injured. Then my husband came out. He was badly beaten. Even now he is still confined to a bed. Then they grabbed me by my hand and took me inside the room. Then they raped me inside the room."

Rufeeda, in her early twenties, said that five soldiers entered her compound and grabbed her and her friend:

"They took us outside the village. I don't know exactly where. We were two and we were taken to the same place. Two of them raped me and my friend was raped by three. They left us out there. [The next morning] my mother and my aunt found us. They took me to our house."

Nur al-Huda, in her early twenties, said soldiers came to her compound on Friday morning, chased away her husband and two of them raped her. She recognized some of the soldiers as belonging to the nearby SAF base.

After being raped she spoke with six of her friends from her neighborhood and learned that they were also raped that morning.

Nadia, in her early twenties, was in her compound on Friday morning cooking breakfast and making food to take to her farm when a group of soldiers arrived, beat the men and raped the women. The soldiers spent several hours in the compound:

Eighteen soldiers came into our house. Three took the men out. They beat the men with the back of their guns. Then they dragged [the men] out of the house. Then the fifteen [remaining soldiers] raped us, all four of us. They beat us and they did whatever they wanted.

Nadia said five other women from the town told her they were also raped on the same day.

Tahira, in her mid-twenties, was alone on Friday morning at about 10.00 a.m., when soldiers attacked her:

"I was in our compound. I heard the noise and came out of our compound. I saw some of [the soldiers] chasing a girl. They arrested her and beat her. ... When they saw me they ran towards me and knocked me down. Then they raped me. They raped me on the street [in front of my house]."

Yasmin, in her early thirties, said she saw a group of soldiers coming towards her house on Friday morning, and ran to her neighbor's house for safety. The soldiers then entered her neighbor's house, found her with women and boys, and raped her. "They hit me with a baton and pointed a gun toward me and made me lie down," she said. "They said I would be killed if I didn't lie down. ... They raped us and we were scared. I am still suffering."

Asal, in her early twenties, said soldiers came into her compound and tied up her brother, hung him from a tree, then raped her, tied her up, and left her:

Three men came inside the hut; two of them held me, while the third raped me. When I cried they pushed a piece of cloth into my mouth. Then the other one raped me. And then they tied me up and left me inside the hut. Then my mother came and untied me and my brother. ... [my mom] cried a lot. Then we all cried.

Asal said that after she was raped her mother treated her "with hot water, in the traditional way," and recalled hearing screams coming from the village all night, which she believes was other victims. After the incident she spoke to two of her neighbors who told her they were also raped on Friday night.

Najma, in her mid-twenties, was in her compound with her two young children when soldiers entered very early Saturday morning. She said:

I was in the bathroom taking a shower. Four soldiers ... found me in the bathroom. ... When I wanted to put on my clothes the soldier stopped me. ... Then they threw me on the ground. Then they raped me. When they finished they threw me in the room and locked me up. Then I heard my neighbors screaming and shouting.

She said she recognized two of her attackers: "I know two of [the attackers]. I know their faces. One was in a military uniform. One was in civilian clothes. They are from the [nearby] garrison."

Khatera, in her early forties, said that soldiers came into her house and raped her and her three daughters, two of whom were under the age of eleven:

Immediately after they entered the room they said: "You killed our man. We are going to show you true hell." Then they started beating us. They took my husband away while beating him. They raped my three daughters and me. Some of them were holding the girl down while another one was raping her. They did it one by one. One helped beat and the other raped. Then they would go to the next girl. Two were holding the girl and one would rape. They put clothes in [their] mouths so that you could not hear the screaming."

Katwoa, in her thirties, told Human Rights Watch that she was with her newborn baby in her compound on Thursday evening when soldiers entered her compound, beat her, then went to the neighbors and raped a girl who was about fifteen-years-old:

"They asked me what I was doing in the house. I told them that I just delivered a baby. They asked me to come out from the room. I refused. ... Then they came and beat me. ... I was injured on my head from a stick. When they beat me they left. They went to my neighbor's house. They beat my neighbors. They raped my neighbor's daughter. ... She is about fifteen."

In some instances, men who were chased away by soldiers returned home to find their daughters had been raped.

Hamid, in his sixties, said that his two eldest daughters, both of whom were under the age of fifteen, and their mother were raped during an attack on his neighborhood on Friday. He told Human Rights Watch that soldiers arrived in his neighborhood at about 8.00 p.m., accused him of being a rebel and killing their comrade, beat him, and beat his sons with whips and chased them out of the compound. As he was being dragged away, he saw soldiers enter the room where his wife and daughters were and heard them screaming.

Ahmed, in his fifties, said that he found his daughters were raped when he returned home after soldiers detained and beat him on Thursday night: "When I came back [home] Friday morning I found women tied up and men tied up and women raped. In my family I have four girls who were raped. One is only fourteen."

In addition to the fifteen rape survivors, Human Rights Watch interviewed twenty one other victims and witnesses to other abuses. These include the use of excessive force, arbitrary arrests and detention, and beatings and other ill-treatment. The soldiers accused many of the men from the town of being rebels, and arrested them or chased out of their compounds. During this time, soldiers remained inside compounds and raped women and girls.

Tasnim, in her forties, heard members of her family and neighbors being raped inside her compound on Friday night. Before the soldiers entered the compound, she hid behind some sacks of millet and firewood, from where she saw her uncle being beaten with a whip and chased out of the compound and heard women screaming. She later learned three women had been raped and a member of her family had been abducted by soldiers and raped.

Tasnim helped to treat many women for injuries resulting from acts of sexual violence. Seven of the women, whom she helped treat, told her that they had been raped.

Tahir, in his twenties, said soldiers beat him severely in his compound on Friday evening. He told Human Rights Watch that during the weeks after the incident he spoke with twelve women from different parts of Tabit who alleged that they were raped on either Thursday or Friday. Overall, Human Rights Watch collected names of 126 rape victims.

Rape and other serious abuses against civilians in Tabit are serious violations of international humanitarian law (the laws of war) and international human rights law. Military personnel who participated in, aided or abetted, or ordered rape are responsible for war crimes. Commanding officers who knew or should have known of the mass rape – and took no action to prevent it or punish those responsible – are criminally liable as a matter of command responsibility.

Since the attacks, Sudanese government officials, military commanders, and traditional leaders responsible for Tabit have taken drastic measures to prevent information about the rapes and other abuses from becoming public. They have threatened intimidated, beaten, detained, and tortured residents of Tabit to prevent them from speaking out about what took place. The authorities have also repeatedly denied UNAMID and other investigators access to the town.

The Sudanese government-appointed Special Prosecutor for Crimes in Darfur visited Tabit on November 20; but amid a large government presence residents were too afraid to report what had occurred and he concluded that no crimes had been committed.

This is a typical example of the cruelty and injustice the people of Sudan faced at the hands of those who were meant to be their leaders and protectors. The violence is appalling and the pain is unbearable. It is almost as if the people are on the run all the days of their lives.

CHAPTER 4:

ADVERSITY AND TRIBULATION

Lord have mercy upon my weary soul
Unto thee I gaze, dear Lord, make me whole
When in adversity, grant me the grace
Thy word have I heeded, show me thy face.

Le Corbeau

In times of great adversity and tribulation, it is easy to feel lost and alone on some forgotten highway travelled by many, but remembered by few. We tend to question everything and everyone, even our faith and our values. In these trying times, there is no person exempt. No one would blame the people of Sudan for bitterness after all they have been through. However, almost none of them have reneged on their trust in Christ. The vast majorities of the Christians in Sudan have, instead, clung fast to their beliefs and today are growing even stronger in the Christian faith. Especially for the people of South Sudan, for a long time they seemed to be fighting to keep the very fabric of their existence. For a prophetic race that had welcomed Christianity with open arms, for a people who seem to have ingrained in their very beings an inexplicable, reflexive love for God, the Sudanese have paid dearly for their faith with much tribulation.

The Ancient Ethiopians, by whom we mean the Cushites, were among the few tribes who stood up for the cause of the Lord. For example, when empire-building

Sennacherib, the Assyrian King, was raising hell and tormenting the children of Israel who were then under the rule of King Hezekiah, it was Tirhakah, the Ethiopian ruler at the time, who stood up to challenge and waged war against him.

According to 2 Kings 19:1-11, "When King Hezekiah heard their report, he tore his clothes and put on burlap and went into the Temple of the Lord. And he sent Eliakim the palace administrator, Shebna the court secretary, and the leading priests, all dressed in burlap, to the prophet Isaiah son of Amoz. They told him, "This is what King Hezekiah says: Today is a day of trouble, insults, and disgrace. It is like when a child is ready to be born, but the mother has no strength to deliver the baby. But perhaps the Lord your God has heard the Assyrian chief of staff, sent by the king to defy the living God, and will punish him for his words. Oh, pray for those of us who are left!" After King Hezekiah's officials delivered the king's message to Isaiah, the prophet replied, "Say to your master, 'this is what the Lord says: Do not be disturbed by this blasphemous speech against me from the Assyrian king's messengers. Listen! I myself will move against him, and the king will receive a message that he is needed at home. So he will return to his land, where I will have him killed with a sword." Meanwhile, the Assyrian chief of staff left Jerusalem and went to consult the king of Assyria, who had left Lachish and was attacking Libnah. Soon afterward King Sennacherib received word that King Tirhakah of Ethiopia was leading an army to fight against him. Before leaving to meet the attack, he sent messengers back to Hezekiah in Jerusalem with this message: "This message is for King Hezekiah of Judah. Don't let your God, in whom you trust, deceive you with promises that Jerusalem will not be captured by the king of Assyria. You know perfectly well what the kings of Assyria have done wherever they have gone. They have completely destroyed everyone who stood in their way! Why should you be any different?"

It is very clear what happened here; Sennacherib had become a bully in his quest to build an empire for himself. He had already been eyeing the Israelites for quite a while. The Israelite King, Hezekiah, did not have sufficient military with which to confront the Assyrian King's intimidating forces. Therefore, Sennacherib fearlessly sent letters containing threats to the Israelite king. King Tirhakah of Ethiopia, however, unfazed by Sennacherib's rough conduct, sent his army to face Sennacherib. It must be remembered that this is the same Tirhakah who conquered Egypt and ruled as one of its first Ethiopian Pharaohs. Tirhakah's brazen confrontation of Sennacherib apparently unnerved the Assyrian king. He resorted to blustering harangues, but could not immediately carry out his threats for fear of being attacked in turn by Tirhakah. Ultimately, the Lord miraculously dispelled the Assyrian threat by way of angelic extermination. Apparently, Tirhakah played a germane role in this conquest; by psychological force instead of brute strength. So, for a people who stood up to the Assyrians when danger faced the children of God, one may be sorely tempted to question why they had to endure so much persecution.

The answer lies in the Bible. The Lord revealed to the Prophet Isaiah what would be the fate of the people of Sudan. In the book of Isaiah 18, the Lord explicitly directed a whole set of prophecies against the Sudanese, describing a great evil that was to befall them and how he would do nothing but watch on while they did to themselves as they willed. According to Isaiah, as inspired by the Lord, "Listen, Ethiopia – land of fluttering sails that lies at the headwaters of the Nile that sends ambassadors in swift boats down the river. Go, swift messengers! Take a message to a tall, smooth-skinned people, who are feared far and wide for their conquests and destruction, and whose land is divided by rivers. All you people of the world, everyone who lives on the earth – when I raise my battle flag on the mountain, look! When I blow the ram's horn, listen! For the Lord has told me this:

"I will watch quietly from my dwelling place – as quietly as the heat rises on a summer day, or as the morning dew forms during the harvest." Even before you begin your attack, while your plans are ripening like grapes, the Lord will cut off your new growth with pruning shears. He will snip off and discard your spreading branches. Your mighty army will be left dead in the fields for the mountain vultures and wild animals. The vultures will tear at the corpses all summer. The wild animals will gnaw at the bones all winter. At that time the Lord of Heaven's Armies will receive gifts from this land divided by rivers, from this tall, smooth-skinned people, who are feared far and wide for their conquests and destruction. They will bring the gifts to Jerusalem, where the Lord of Heaven's Armies dwell."

This Ethiopian river is in modern day Bible translations written as the rivers of Cush and is now referred to as the Upper Nile. These people have been feared far and wide and have always been aggressive people. Concerning their speech, it must have been, to the Prophet Isaiah, a strange tongue because it was not among the languages familiar to the Israelites at that time. This prophecy came to the people of Sudan after they had – under King Tirhaka – (who was both king to the Cushites and pharaoh to the Egyptians) repelled the forces of Sennacherib from the Israeli borders. By means of this prophecy, therefore, we are made to understand that while the horrors and troubles the Sudanese have faced is a direct result of certain man-made woes – ranging from religious bigotry and ethnic jingoism to oil disputes and the general corruption of avaricious leaders – these occurrences should really not seem so strange, because they have already been predicted in the Bible and are just now coming to fulfillment.

CHAPTER 5:

YOUR SONS AND DAUGHTERS SHALL PROPHESY

What the future holds, man oft never
knows Alas fate, destiny; man's freedom's woes,
Twin streams which from
Predestination flows God always to his
Faithful Prophet shows.

Le Corbeau.

Perhaps foremost and most indelible in the memories of the people of Sudan is the story of Prophet Zacharia Biar Atem. He was one of the few prophets who actually would see things happen before they happened. In some cases, much like the prophets of old, he would even receive solutions to the problems, which he would follow to the letter. It was one of these encounters with God that brought him in contact with Jerry Drino who published his encounter with Zacharia Biar Atem on the Episcopal church of Sudan's website:

"Zacharia Biar Atem, priest and prophet of the Diocese of Bor in Sudan once relayed to me that as a young boy he received a vision while caring for cattle. A great wind entered him, and he began to sing in a language he did not know. He then had a vision of a great disaster falling upon southern Sudan and that everything was destroyed, including the church. He returned to his village to tell the people that these things would come to pass. This was in 1980. When the second civil war came in 1983, he said that he could not escape into the bush, but had to be in the front lines of the Sudanese People's Liberation Army. God continued to stir prophecies within him, he said, and he advised chiefs and commanders and bishops of what God was directing them to do.

During some of the fiercest fighting in Bor Town, he said God told him he must go into the town center and nail three flags to a tree to stop the fighting. He said that despite the fact his body filled with fear, he did it. As bullets flew, he prayed that he would die quickly, rather than having to suffer. He nailed the flags to the tree, and the fighting stopped. Zacharia was in Ethiopia with the so-called Lost Boys and Girls. He had a dream that they all would be forced to flee back to Sudan and eventually to Kenya. In his dream, a pregnant woman fell in front of him and began to give birth. Because there were no other women nearby, he had to help deliver twins. In 1991, the Ethiopian army started to raid the refugee camps, and all fled back to the Sudan. As Zacharia was running, a pregnant woman did fall before him and started to give birth, just as his dream had told him. He helped her two sons come into the world.

In November 2004, he had another vision that he must find a crippled priest to deliver a message. He would tell him that what he was doing to help rebuild the communities in the Diocese of Bor would be blessed by God. According to the vision, he would find the priest with a man from another country who did not speak Dinka. He would bring a shirt with a particular design, and this would be the sign. He was to tell this man what God wanted him to do in Sudan. Zacharia walked more than 1,000 miles, first to Uganda and then to Kenya, in search of two men whom he did not know.

In Nairobi, the crippled priest, Canon Mark Atem Thuc, was told that Zacharia was searching for him, but that he should be wary of him and should not be trusted.

"No," Mark said, "he is a child of God, and we will not turn him away."

In 2005 Abuna Zachariah was living with Mark and his family in a tiny two-room space. I [Jerry] had brought T-shirts from my former parish with a shield-design on them. Three days later, in Kakuma Refugee Camp, Zacharia took me aside with an interpreter and for the next four hours relayed his story and what God had told him to tell me. He told me of the vision three months earlier, and how he saw the shirts in his vision.

At the end he said, "You remember the woman that I dreamed of and that actually gave birth to twins? I met her recently. She was so happy to see me and told me that her sons were strong and well. She said that she wanted to give me two cattle in thanksgiving for what I did. I must now give you one of these cattle because I have told you what God wanted me to deliver, and my burden has been lifted.

"The cattle are in the Sudan, but here is the halter which carries the soul of the cattle. Ask the boys back in San Jose, and they will tell you what it means. I have now told you want you must do. I am free."

Much recently, South Sudan was set agog by a very popular man of God, Abraham Chol, who prophesied against the General Chief of Staff of SPLA, warning him to either give up fighting against him, or risk his job and even his life. It was not just a simple threat of prophetic power, yet, nobody took his words seriously. Days later, Gen. Malong Awan, critically sick, was rushed to Jordan seeking medical attention. The incident was widely received with fear and trust in the man of God. Abraham Chol is known generally in south Sudan and Juba, in particular, for his vigorously vehement language against the evil practices in the country, and his followers are not limited to his clan, but are actually spread across the country. His past predictions against General Paul Malong Awan, and their eventual fulfillment is an indication of the amount of attention and respect he has garnered.

There is yet another interesting case of a prophet. His name is Isaac Pal Mun. Among the South Sudanese who have faced so much war and displacement, knowing one's birth date is an important factor that goes a long way in easing the process of emigration and immigration. Isaac Pal Mun was born in 1972 in the town of Yoy. He is one of the foremost and fiercest prophets in the Sudan. Elbow Chuol of Nyamile documents a bit about the life of Isaac Pal Mun. His message may astound many due to the simplicity inherent in it, yet it is oftentimes these simple messages that get overlooked and underestimated in favor of the complex ones. The simple message was; "Repent and God will have mercy on you." Such a thing like "repentance" would seem exceedingly trivial to the ears of the listeners.

The prophet loved to wear a black T-shirt with a large and boldly engraved clause; "Jesus Saves." His prophecies were limited only to disasters that would or were about to befall the country. He was always armed with his Bible on his right hand, and Israeli flag on his other hand. Whether or not he took the vow of the Nazarite is a mystery to many, for his beard, quite unshaven kept growing and shooting out. He derives a sort of serenity from walking everywhere, preaching the message of God. Whenever he made an appearance, people would gather around him, and would get to hear mostly the most interesting things. He believed he saw everything about the current crisis in South Sudan already and would keep prophesying about them. Isaac Pal Mun is a normal man whose words never go unfulfilled. He is from Eastern Jikany Nuer, growing up in the Southeastern part of the Sudan now literally referred to as Eastern Upper Nile in South Sudan. According to his acceptances, he is a poor man who never dreams of building or stocking up wealth, but his riches are built upon the words of the living God, the God of Israel.

Just like Abraham Chol, Isaac is highly confident that the almighty God of Heaven has appointed him to preach the message to South Sudanese about the fate patiently awaiting them. Back in the days, Mr Pal was a normal man running his business activities between the borders of Ethiopia and South Sudan. That was more than 15 years ago. Dreams began appearing to him when he was 28 years old, and the first vision he received was that he was going to Israel in the near future to lift up the banner of South Sudan on the Mount Zion. "God told me I will be going to Holy Land to lift up the banner which prophet Isaiah prophesied more 3,000 years before Christ. And when I informed people about this, they told me to see the doctor that I was now going crazy talking of the things which can never be true." Prophet Isaac announced the good news, and six years later, extrasensory Isaac would make it to the Holy Land, only to spend a few years and then return home.

He was the only man in existence who made it to Mount Zion purposely sent by God to lift up the flag of the newest nation on earth. The task was not as easy as he had hoped; he was sometimes beaten, and he would go a day or night without food just like the old bystander prophets. "I have evidences that Jehovah appointed me as the next prophet to the South Sudanese after Ngundeng." The name Ngundeng Bong is one of the most criticized by Christians in Western Gambella, alongside those in Nasir. They do not like Isaac mentioning Ngundeng in his preaching, which they consider contradictory to his claims, because many people perceived

Ngundeng as an evil agent who never fit in the Christian faith. But prophet Isaac Pal Mun believed Ngundeng was like any other prophet that ever walked the earth, partially because most of his predications came true.

Historically it seems people are automatically opposed to other's affirmations about the hidden mysterious typecasts in the dark world. Perhaps because these prophets are normal men and women living amongst us; they possess an amazing power that the average man cannot fathom – the skill to foretell tomorrow's events. In early June 2001, Isaac saw a tarmac road all the way from Gambella, passing through Kuergeng (Lare). When he told people about his vision, the very next day some powerful men in the authority decided to challenge his prediction. They mocked him and embarrassed him, doing all but arresting him. Accusing him of being mad, they said he was fitting to remove his clothes and commence walking naked. Of course, Isaac disputed the notion of one being mad.

"You can tell a mad man by the following; a mad man walks naked or with dirty clothes probably collecting them from the garbage. These mad men attain incoherence in whatever it is they say. They can say anything without knowing they say it. Third, a mad person stays where he is not accepted". Isaac then asked, "Now are you seeing these things in me?"

He is in fact a very normal man. Nine years later, Kuergeng hosts one of the smoothest tarmac roads in Western Ethiopia.

In another prophecy made by Isaac – Thoorbadak in Nyieninyang, Western Ethiopia of Gambella, was one time an odd place where hundreds of people got killed by Nuer rebels. Isaac announced in the same year that it would be one day a big market with the people around this place enjoying and living peacefully. Now it is. There are buildings, markets, and cars, which 15 years ago was not even imaginable.

Prophet Isaac announced that the Nuer in Israel will be deported back to their country. Months later, the president of South Sudan, Salva Kiir Mayardit signed a diplomatic package requesting the government of Israel to return the illegal immigrants back to their home country. Within the same year, hundreds of South Sudanese, mostly Nuer ethnics were flushed back to the country's capital, Juba. Isaac was among the victims. For those who have heard the message, his prophecies came to pass.

In 2013, upon his return from Jerusalem, Isaac prophesied of impending disaster while at Jebel church, Juba, South Sudan. It was on Sunday, three days prior to the removal of long time serving South Sudanese Vice President, Dr. Riek Machar. The mass which was officially attended by some of the most dignified other politicians. Isaac announced the disaster. "Juba is going to be on fire. People are going to kill each other in this city. Some people in fact will be staying outside the big towns in our nation."

"I can also see famine and diseases coming into this nation. All these things will take place because God sent me to proclaim this truth and people should begin to repent from their sins. Amongst this practice is, too much drinking from top leadership to the simple men and women in the farm yards in Juba city." (By this, he meant there was a lot of corruption, money laundering, and embezzlement going on.) "Secondly, there is an increase of prostitution in this town, and God is not pleased about this immorality. Thirdly...." The microphone was swiftly taken away before concluding by Kok Ruei. His prophecy was immediately rejected.

Isaac was disappointed. No one feels more pain than a rejected prophet. He is among the unwanted. He is not even welcome in his own home. "The crisis in south Sudan will come to an end this year". He continues referring to this year, 2015. He says; "God is not happy with the death in this chosen nation. He told me, if it is about peace let all South Sudanese focus on peace instead of war. If they choose guns, one party would this year, be defeated for good and the whole thing will finally be off." He also warns that, "if South Sudanese leaders will not compromise for the sake of peace, something terrible is going to happen to some of them."

There is another Prophet whose inspiration to make prophecies is very controversial. He is one of the earliest prophets in Sudan's recent history; his name is Ngundeng Bong. Many called him a charlatan, but his prophecies seemed to carry a lot of weight. Douglas H. Johnson, in his article states, "What did Ngundeng really do?" articulated Ngundeng Bong's life and some of his prophecies. Ngundeng claimed to speak with the voice of Deng – a divine figure known to both Nuer and Dinka and to many people throughout the Upper Nile basin. As a prophet of Deng he addressed many issues affecting the social cohesion of Nuer society, and Nuer relations with their neighbors as well. He opposed the use of private magic for personal gain, so much so that he banished his eldest son for dabbling in it. He condemned both inter-sectional feuds among the Nuer and cattle raids against the Dinka – something that the British, who were no friends of Ngundeng, later confirmed.

But the paradox of Ngundeng as a prophet of peace was that he secured his reputation through victory in a major battle. In about 1879 the Lou Nuer were attacked by a coalition of Dinka and Gaawar Nuer, led by an ex-soldier from the Egyptian army (he was described as being circumcised and carrying a sword or bayonet), but Ngundeng decisively defeated them at Pading, near Khor Fulus [Dinka for pul luth or mud fish pond]. Some of the earliest recorded eyewitness accounts of this battle indicate that Ngundeng laid an ambush for the invading force and pushed them back into the swampy area where they were defeated. Later versions, however, attribute his victory entirely to his spiritual power. In these versions Ngundeng killed his attackers through the power of his decorated stick – the dang (rod or baton). He raised it to the sky, invoked his divinity, and his enemies died.

The problem with gaining an early reputation for military victory is that people expect you to repeat it. When a British-led armed column approached Ngundeng's village in 1902 the Lou expected him to repeat his victory at Pading. Ngundeng raised his dang, announced that his divinity was not present, and disbanded his force. Whether Ngundeng acted through divine inspiration, or he made a shrewd assessment of the chances of the spear-armed Nuer against the rifle-armed soldiers of the Anglo-Egyptian army, we will never know for sure. The soldiers demonstrated their specific intentions by burning down Ngundeng's village and confiscating the ivory tusks surrounding his shrine.

By refusing to fight, Ngundeng avoided the fate that finally befell his son Guek Ngundeng in 1929. When the government of the day accused Guek of plotting a rebellion, he at first tried to evade the army but was rebuked by his age-mate, who claimed that if Ngundeng were alive he would have defeated the army just like he had defeated his foes at Pading. When Guek finally confronted the Sudan Defense Force in front of his father's shrine and tried to re-enact his father's famous victory, he was shot dead along with a number of his followers, and his body was hung from a tree for all to see his fate.

But before I present more of the North-South relations, let me present a few of the South Sudan internal affairs, particularly some of the positive and less sensitive ones. And let me refer you to some of the following names which

Ngundeng used in his songs, which readers may come across in the article. Yang (cow), Luak (byre) and Wec (country), they can all refer to South Sudan as used by Ngundeng. Hok (cattle) and raan (person), naath (people) can all refer to people in his usage. There is a saying in Nuer that "Raan e yang kuoth" meaning "Man or human being is a cow of God." Also Ngundeng used nicknames for himself and for other people he mentioned. For example, Jambiel (colorful), Mac Thok (language grabber), etc. are nicknames he used to describe himself. By Jambiel he likened himself to a beautiful color. People also say he used the name Mac Thok because he could understand languages of strangers.

Elders say Ngundeng predicted some of our present leaders. In his songs he talked of a leader called 'Kiir Nyal Diing' who would lead our people. Elders say it is Salva Kiir Mayardit. The name 'Kiir' would match the first name of our current leader, but 'Nyal Diing' is just a nickname describing Kiir. 'Nyal Diing' in Nuer are names of many doted colours, for example like that of a cow and leopard, etc. It simply translates "Kiir of many colors." Ngundeng said this Kiir will one day bring, probably bad news, to his people when he said "Kiir Nyal Dieng be ha juoc lom." Literally translates "Kiir Nyal Diing will bring me messages." But the word 'lom' in Nuer is more of a 'gossip' than just a message or news. And in what form will he bring the news, nobody knows.

Ngundeng also said "Tik yual kuoth bi mac de bool." This translates "The flames of fire of the God's long bearded man shall be widespread." Some elders say he meant our late hero Dr. John Garang de Mabior in reference to the magnitude and severity of the 21 years of the wide spread civil war in the South which he led. Others think it is also Salva Kiir. Ngundeng also talked of the current South Sudan Vice President, Dr. Riek Machar among other leaders, some of whom are either dead and others alive, and others with names that are not clear to me because of nicknames.

Ngundeng, after prophesying a lot of suffering and internal fighting among South Sudanese, finally predicted a unified South Sudan under a loving and caring leadership. He predicted a happy people that would not recognize themselves on the basis of tribalism. It is not yet clear whether this predicted unity is supposed to happen before or after independence. In his songs in Nuer he said, "Cia ben pal gaat ka diaal e nga bi nga ngico, cang ni Ngok bike toang cuare dual ke beri marol; gueth ce jany ke ram kel ce bi yic ni how; jiok nyal yith tung de puar; ci gueth jany ke rol mac ce bi yic ni how; jiok nyal yith tung de puar."

It translates: "You have all come together, praying together all my children without bothering to know who is who; even the Ngok will participate in the building (of the nation); don't be afraid of Jalaba's flags; the power has been in one person, but this will not be too confusing for the world (nation?); my colored bull's long horns reach to the skies; the power has lasted long with Jalaba, but will not be too confusing for the world; my colored bull's long horns reach to the skies."

Since this sounds like a political statement in regard to the North-South relations, elders recalled Ngundeng's explanations that it may mean unity of the people of South Sudan. They also say that he predicts how powerful or rich South Sudan would be when he likened it to a bull with long horns that reach to the skies. They compared this to a description in the Bible in which God described a once powerful Kingdom of Nebuchadnezzar to a big tree with long branches under which all kinds of birds rest. And again, Ngundeng refers to South Sudan as a cow or in this case, a bull. In economic sense he describes it as a cow that produces milk (resources) and in the sense of political or military power he describes it as a bull with long horns.

It also said "Nuer yiene Jang cang loke haa be ngoang e ba dhile guurun." Translation, "Nuer and Dinka, even if you dislike or reject me, I will still be your father someday." It is sometimes confusing to try to know who Ngundeng refers to when he says 'I', because he seems to represent everybody of his choice in South Sudan. Readers will notice that in the following paragraphs he seems to say 'I' as a representative of everything from God, himself and the leader of the South.

He continued to say "gook nyaliep, gook nyaliep cuare kuar kuon ruac Deng rol kene wea (cuor) ka jala ke mac mi riaw how." It translates "Prophets (leaders?); prophets of Nyaliep don't reject the leader; God rules the land with vultures and I am carrying a weapon that lightens the skies." Again, I don't know who he refers to by the name 'Nyaliep' that has prophets (leaders) who he cautioned not to reject the leader. And who is that leader? The elders I asked did not know.

In what seems to be his assurances, Ngundeng said "Jal Deng ke mac mi riaw how, chan dial bi ku kaan ke Ngundeng, Ngundeng Bong laar jiak ka laar goy, cuara beera mat keel kene beer roal...luore cier e bee mo ...e hoo ruac kuar ke nei ti mieng, ca laat caara cu pal ruec." He says "God holds a weapon that lightens the skies (world); all the poor will survive because of Ngundeng; Ngundeng Bong says bad things and also says good things; don't mix my flag with the flag of Jalaba...receive the star from the East....It is because the leader talks to the deaf, who have forgotten the messages of the black (cow)". Again, here he refers to prophesies about South Sudan as prophesies about a black cow. He warned against combining the flag of Jalaba and that of his (South Sudan). It is not clear to elders what he meant by mixing of flags. Some say he might have meant the current GONU and

GOSS flags used by Salva Kiir. Others also think that two different flags could simply symbolize his declaration of separation (two separate independent countries).

Ngundeng also predicted the return of his dang (rod), which was taken to South Sudan from Great Britain after 80 years, when he said in his song, "Mi ciaa thuok ke ruac noonge dang, en mac thok eni nyuura." This translates, "If you have finished with the talks (debates) bring my rod (dang); I, the language grabber, am still seated." Elders say the timing of return of Ngundeng's rod was in accordance with his prediction. Some say the talks could mean the Naivasha peace talks in Kenya. Others think it means the current debates going on in the implementation of the CPA. But they all agree that the return of dang symbolizes the return of power, which they said was lost since 1920s, or acquisition of modern weaponry. He also said "Kuar dang nguan ngot ni joor jal ke jur ti kur ke bathdor ...bi wang cuec de a cang kene pay." It translates "Four leaders are yet to come with hundreds and thousands of strangers (forces)...on my right eye will be sun and moon." Elders think that these hundreds and thousands of strangers that are yet to come may mean foreign forces of aggression against South Sudan by about four countries. But Ngundengsaid they would also be defeated. Again, this is a food for thought.

Another prophesy that elders think is directly related to the people of Southern Blue Nile is when Ngundeng said in his songs "Lare Funj ci maar e dan daak, kua lar Funj, lare je co nyal kua lat ke leer." It says "Tell the Funj that the past relations have ended; tell Funj, tell the son-in-law; continue to discuss it over." This to elders is also confusing. Some think the prophesy talks of ending past relations between Funj and Jalaba or may be ending relations between Funj and South Sudan. And who is the 'son-in-law' in this case, is also confusing. And what does it mean to say 'continue to talk it over?'

I have not come across anything that mentions Nuba Mountains or its people. It could be in a different tape. Or I might have not understood that he meant Nuba Mountains, if he used some kind of a nickname for the region.

These are again some of the songs I noted. I could not present most of them. The whole cassette can nearly take a hundred pages if I were to transcribe it all. The songs were not recorded directly from the mouth of Ngundeng himself for those of you who need some clarity. There was no tape recorder in Nuerland, at least during Ngundeng's lifetime. But those who were with him passed the message in form of songs which were easily remembered and recorded after the benefit of the tape recorder technology reached the Nuerland. My cassette was recorded in 1988 by a different fellow who went to Wec Deang (Lou-Nuer) and recorded it from a grandson of Ngundeng Bong. I then recorded it from him in 1992. But it is always the same even if you record it from different Nuer elders in Unity, Upper Nile and Jonglei states. They may differ in the order of the songs' tracks, but the songs will remain the same.

I understand that it is not easy to correctly interpret what Ngundeng really said about Sudan. Even Nuer elders continue to struggle to find the correct interpretations. This is the reason they prefer to wait for their occurrence to just fit them into things that have already passed and getting to pass. For example, if you asked a Nuer elder just in 1988, the time my cassette was originally recorded, he would not explain to you what Ngundeng meant by "Wii Wal" (ten states). He would just get confused because at that time there were only three regions of Equatoria, Bahr el Ghazal and Upper Nile in the South in 1988. But after the present government of Omer el Bashir divided the South into ten states in 1993, elders then rushed to confirm that these were the ten states Ngundeng predicted.

There was also the tragic death of Dr. John Garang de Mabior. I heard about his predicted fate by Ngundeng from about three different elders. One told me about it since 1988 that there was something Ngundeng said about Dr. Garang. Again after he signed the CPA, and before he could take oath of office as First Vice President of Sudan and President of the Government of Southern Sudan, two other elders told me that unless Ngundeng was wrong in his prophesies, Dr. Garang would not live longer after entering Khartoum. When I heard about his death over the news I felt shocked and afraid. I couldn't believe it. I couldn't believe that what the elders told me could come true.

I came to realize that Ngundeng could be right in his prophesies. He might have been empowered with vision by God to tell us about events that were going to happen. This could be the reason why he claimed to have been given "God's eye glasses." I think he meant he was empowered with God's vision to enable him see into the future with accuracy.

However, I still stand with my word that I would NEVER agree with anybody who tries to make people believe that Ngundeng is God that can be worshipped. No, that can be a big mistake; even Ngundeng himself would have opposed it. To me, he was simply a prophet or messenger of God; as simple as that.

Whether their prophecies are of the Lord or not is a matter for serious debate. We do know, however, that the Lord promised that the sons and daughters of our lands will prophecy... a prophecy on its own that is fast becoming a reality in Sudan.

CHAPTER 6:

ON THE RUN

*No adversity should you fear for He
whom you serve has from bondage set
you free by divine virtue of his stripes,
you're healed trust, and you will to
Heaven's will be sealed.*

Le Corbeau

Growing up in Bor, Kuol had always been fascinated by the stories of Christ and the Late Arch Deacon Archibald Shaw, the Macour of Dinka. This is the way the people of Dinka sometimes name certain warriors in their tribe. Archibald Shaw was a pioneer missionary with the Gordon Memorial Sudan mission of the Church Missionary Society. The first modern Christian mission was established by him in December 1905 in Malek. The town of Malek is a small settlement about nineteen kilometers from Bor, where the first primary school was founded by Archibald Shaw. This important school produced the first Anglican Bishop, Reverend Daniel Deng Atong. Unlike many white men, even though Archibald was born English, and was by origin and citizenship English, his discovery of the Lord Jesus Christ, and his subsequent love for Christ made him possess such a deep care and affection for Africans. It is this love that fueled his work, and gave him continued inspiration for his mission in Sudan.

The Dinka people, who were, and still are an honest tribe of people, also loved him intensely because he helped so many build up their Christian faith, and, he also helped them to maintain steadfastness in the worship of the Lord. One of such people is Kuol. Even though he was born some two years after the Arch Deacon Archibald Shaw passed away, the stories were still being told, and the motivational and astounding legacy left behind by Shaw inspired him. Kuol attended the primary school in Malek shortly after he lost his father, who had died earlier in his life from a bullet wound He was shot in the head when it was discovered by the soldiers that he lied, saying he had no son. During that time, the soldiers were looking for young boys to conscript into their ignominious child-army. His father had hidden both his mother and him, and distracted the soldiers after asking them both to flee to Malek. The sound of a bullet was all he heard as they were meters away from the house. The loss of his father had made his mother weep bitterly. She had heard the gunshot and was sorely tempted to run back to her husband, but she remembered his words, and took her son to safety. He was ten years old at the time, and was very scared. He held his mother's hands as they fled. When they arrived at the camp, tired and hungry with very sore feet, it was Reverend Daniel that received them.

They had told him their unfortunate story and he had been very sympathetic towards them. He made sure they were bathed, fed, and given medicines and a bed they could sleep on for the night. He promised they would get clothes by the next day. Kuol remembered how he had joined other boys in school there at Malek, for by that time, Malek was a stronghold for missionary activity in the upper Nile region. He learned more and more about the person they called their Lord, Jesus Christ of Nazareth, and his works. He learned how Jesus Christ was a genius from a tender age, and how he healed a dove. Kuol had always wished he could heal Sudan. His young mind had not fully being able to fathom the nuances of war and why men even fought them at all. Every night before he slept, and in the morning as soon as he woke, he would go down on his knees to pray to this God (whom they had claimed was the father of this Jesus Christ and would listen to all prayers as far as they were prayed in Jesus' name) about the well-being of Sudan, and for his mother.

His mother suffered and grieved every single day. She was a really strong woman, and even though most times she tried really hard to hide it from the world, through the façade, there was deep pain. He also grieved as a child for his father; he had always seen his father as his personal hero and that was what he was till death. Adding to this pain is the fact that they were unable to bury his father in the respectful way that was befitting for such a responsible man who labored hard for his family all the time. He rarely ever bought anything for himself, but always ensured his family never lacked anything. As far as they were happy, he was. Not that he was the richest man around though, but he knew how to take care of his family, and that was the most important thing.

At the camp, Kuol would study the Bible under the amiable supervision of one of the 'sons' of Archibald Shaw. Although Archibald never got married, he had a humanitarian knack that prompted him to repeatedly adopt Dinka boys who had no family at all. In that regard, he had quite a number of sons. By the time Kuol reached twenty years of age, he already knew from the depths of his heart that he was also going to go into missionary work, and preach the gospel of Christ, so he prepared himself day and night, in thought, words, and deeds, and prayed for God's direction on the right path. By this time, the first civil war had come to a tense and suspicious end, so there was an air of uncertainty about the future. The tension was not totally gone, but the killing had reduced drastically, and people were allowed to feel a bit safe and their worship of God grew stronger.

After he was baptized by John Aruor, Kuol would go out for Evangelism with the group. He went back to Bor at the age of twenty eight. When he arrived there, he started a ministry and became a pastor. Initially, he had just a small amount of people, as some were too scared to come out to worship in the open, choosing rather to worship in secret. It seemed to them that he was still young, and brimming with naiveté. It seemed he did not know what evils had transpired in the general area of South Sudan. He would learn, they figured. They just hoped it wouldn't be the hard way. After two to three years the church increased in size, faith and strength. In 1991 another civil war started again, termed the Bor Massacre where Christians were killed, women were raped, and not even children were spared. Even though many churches were burnt down, this looked like there was more than religious bigotry afoot. It seemed like the intent was to wipe out the entire town of Bor. So many fled the church and town, to look for safety, but Kuol and some other pastors and members remained to pray with those left behind, and also for God's direction.

One Sunday morning after a glorious service and worship in the presence of the Lord, a regiment of soldiers came to terrorize the people of Bor. Children were running down the streets shouting "tulung!" (help!), people running and crying "Teumalireurangbapanasawarga!" (Heavenly Father doesn't ignore us!) Some of Kuol's comrades could not bear the tension anymore, they rushed the prayer and said to Kuol; "Kami barisrengsesholatsakumaha nu ayeunaurangngajalankeun..." (We will finish the prayer as we run...) They ran out and left Kuol on his knees. He could neither blame nor judge them, their flesh was very scared. Kuol looked up to the heavens and cried to God, for wisdom and for his will to be done in his life and their town.

The rebels bashed into the church, and looked around, and one of them noticed Kuol on his knees praying and he said

"Jelema nu bolero, manéhnatahajudbarikotanyadinaseuneu" (fool, he prays while his town is on fire). Kuol didn't fret neither did he stop praying. "Gugah, Sidekuhareupeun kerning Meureunkuringbakalmaehananjeunleuwihlaun" he laughs (get up, kneel before me, maybe I will kill you slowly), the soldier laughed loudly. He loved killing, it was meat he used to kill initially before he was later conscripted into the army because of his exceeding talents at killing. He knew just the right amount of pressure to use when cutting the jugular such that the person would spend such a long time choking before eventually dying. Kuol did not move, he did not say a word; he just knelt there and shut the world out. The rebel was angered. He had never met such insolence in his killing sprees. He was used to seeing even pastors trembling before his angry countenance while he dispatched them quickly with a knife wound to the throat. That was his signature move; the knife to the throat. He moved towards Kuol and pulled him up by his shirt, he kicked Kuol in the behind, Kuol fell back and hit his head against a stone. This injury caused his head to commence bleeding profusely. Kuol pressed his hands against his bleeding head, and kept praying within him. The pain was immense. Another one of the rebels moved towards them and said to his partner and more sadistic comrade in crime and in arms; "IeupisannekadHayuurangngajarkeunmanéhnapalajaran" (this one is stubborn, let's teach him a lesson).

The other rebel had always looked up to the sadistic one as a mentor even though the sadistic one was younger than the mentee, perhaps for the singular reason that the sadistic one was a stone cold murderer and could kill the air if it displeased him. To impress the sadistic rebel, the other slammed the bottom of his rifle against Kuol's head and his unconscious body fell to the floor. Kuol woke up with his vision blurry, he could not even see properly, it was pitch black. For a moment, he thought he had lost his eyesight. He turned his head and looked around; the only light he could behold was a distant light in the sky, the moon. He stretched his hands towards the sky, hot tears burnt his cheeks and he cried; "Forsake uranghenteu, Gusti" (forsake us not Lord), and he fainted again. A very loud noise woke Kuol from his very deep sleep, he jerked up in fear, wondering where the noise came from. He managed to open his eyes only to be greeted with a stinging headache. He squinted and noticed he was in a cage-like prison with some other people. He wondered whether they wanted to use him for sport. He took stock of his environs and noticed that one of them had been beheaded quite recently. The blood was clotting, but the fingers were still twitching and palpitating in final death throes. The people in the prison were crying most piteously at the gory sight, with fear that the hour of their own perdition was at hand.

Kuol looked around and could very well smell the fear in the air: the doubts, the pain, and the anguish. He had forgotten about his wound until a fly perched on his head. He touched the wound and noticed the blood around it had begun to fester and clot simultaneously. One of the inmates walked towards him and said, "Welcome brother, I feared you would die from that wound that no one has attended to, but I guess God is on your side. Although, you may soon be wishing you had died from that wound instead of at the hands of these merciless beasts."

He did not know how to respond so he just said, "How long have I been out?"

The other man told him he was out for two days and on one of those days, he was hallucinating and even begging an individual (whom apparently none but him could see) to take him along. The man said he had been in and out of consciousness and muttering things in his sleep. "I'm Pastor Teng," the man introduced himself, and Kuol did likewise.

Pastor Teng told him how he got there, and how the rebels had captured the others too. He mentioned how his fellow friends in the Lord were locked up in the church and set on fire, and then they were made to listen to their screams as they were burned alive. Kuol was so heartbroken when he heard the gory details. Ten described how they were using the prisoners as sport. The rebels tortured most of them to death, while some they decided to set ablaze. The others were just simply killed directly. They did not feed them, and when they decided to do so, it was with rotten food. Kuol wondered how some people could be so wicked and heartless; and not even just that, they were deploying their heartlessness into debauched practices; killing their fellow countrymen and raping their young girls to death.

Apparently the man that was beheaded previously was the senior brother to the one who had been crying most profusely of the lot. They did not only attack Christians, but also townspeople that did not support their line of action, and those two brothers were a pair of such a case. Kuol managed to get to his feet, and went to look outside; he had to take his eyes off the headless body lying on the floor. He turned to the other men to greet them all. Kuol thought to himself, seeing as that was the likely fate they were all bound to face, there was no need being scared because doing so would not help their situation; neither would it obtain the mercy of their captors. In fact, it would fuel their masochism. As he finished greeting them and going back to his seat, the cell door was opened again, the men cried in horror, and some ran behind others so they would not be picked. They pushed a man in who had obviously been beaten terribly, he fell to the ground, and then one of the rebels threw his Bible at his head and spat on him. Pastor Kuol and Pastor Teng helped him to his feet, (Teng immediately recognizing him as a pastor). They did their introductions and he described how he was captured, how they butchered his wife because he refused to denounce Christ. He was made to watch as they killed her slowly. His children had escaped, all except the baby that was still breast feeding. They yanked the baby off his wife's back and threw him into the fire.

He was very weak because he had been through an incredible lot. He could not hold back the tears that rolled down his cheeks. He was too weak to weep. Both Pastor Kuol and Pastor Teng tried very hard to console him, but was there really a way to? There is no consoling the rivers, the seas, the oceans, the tidal waves, when the moon is removed and the sky is blackened.

Darkness came and the three held hands together to pray before sleeping in different corners on the cold floor. Kuol thought about all the massacres till he dozed off, but just before sleep overtook him, he remembered the naïve prayer he used to make in those days, when he was still a young lad, asking God for the power to heal his country. He thought to himself that he could continue the work of the Lord in their captivity, and convert those who have not been converted, so they could be saved even when calamity fell upon them.

The next morning he told the two pastors his thoughts from the previous night, which they also agreed to. The cell door was opened again. This time water was brought for them, unclean though, but even so it was luxury for every one of them to be able to quench their thirsts. The water brought strength to the three of them. They sat in a circle and started clapping and singing unto God, after a while they stood up and danced as well. Other people in the cell started wondering why they seemed so happy. The rebels heard them and also wondered why there was so much noise. They were irritated by it so they went to the cell. Even when the rebels came in the three pastors didn't stop their worship and dancing. This angered the rebels more, they dragged them outside tied them to a stake and flogged them intensively. After the flaying of their skins, they poured alcohol on their backs to torture them more, but even in their weak states, the three of them continued to pray. The rebels threw them inside the cell again and all three of them crawled to their different corners, said their prayers, and gave into sleep. They woke up the next day with their goals strengthened. They prayed harder than ever, and even their cell mates felt that the three men had death wishes and were in fact, trying to get themselves killed. They started the main goal: preaching the gospel. At first many people did not want to yield. They were wondering what benefits would derive from serving this God when those that had been serving Him for a long time could not be delivered from this predicament.

However, soon afterwards they began to listen when they saw the conviction and passion the pastors had as they preached the gospel. They ministered and shared the good news of our Lord Jesus Christ even though they were in pain. The prisoners watched as the pastors gave their all, even when they had lost everything, and were about to lose their lives as well. It was probably a fulfillment of the words of the Lord in the book of Matthew 5:13-16; "You are the salt of the earth. But what good is salt if it has lost its flavor? Can you make it salty again? It will be thrown out and trampled underfoot as worthless. You are the light of the world – like a city on a hilltop that cannot be hidden. No one lights a lamp and then puts it under a basket. Instead, a lamp is placed on a stand, where it gives light to everyone in the house. In the same way, let your good deeds shine out for all to see, so that everyone will praise your heavenly Father."

The prisoners listened and most of them gave their lives to Christ, some even asked to be baptized. Two weeks after this, the rebels announced that they were going to release some of the people.

Those remaining would be killed. Kuol and his comrades held hands; at least they would die on Christ. On the day of release the rebel pointed to Kuol as he was picking people to free. At first he was shocked. And then later, Pastor Teng was also called out. They were very surprised at the turn out; it seemed the rebels had mistakenly released them. Kuol and Teng looked at the third pastor, giving him a sincere look to remain strong; he would not be going with them.

Kuol returned to the area he was captured, to see if he can revive what was left of his ministry. To date, he still preaches the gospel. The Lord has been with him and he continues worshipping the Lord in spirit and in truth. This is why the apostle Paul in his second letter to Timothy said; "I have fought the good fight, I have finished the race, and I have remained faithful. And now the prize awaits me – the crown of righteousness, which the Lord, the righteous Judge will give me on the day of his return. And the prize is not just for me but for all who eagerly look forward to his appearing."

CHAPTER 7:

STAND YOUR GROUND

Once, we were one; of our ancestor Cush,
and then we were two, we started to push
each other aside for what we know not,
stay your sword, I'll stay mine –
Let peace be our lot.

Le Corbeau

There is the popular story of a professor who carried out an experiment in his sociology class; or is it a philosophy class? Ah, yes, it was a theology class. Well, the following account really happened in one of these classes, and what happened is as follows. The professor, trying to prove a point on humanism and the importance of human beings helping one another, collected the identity cards of all the students in the class and put them in a bag. There were around one hundred and twenty students. He then placed the bag in front of the class and afterwards announced to them that anyone who was able to find his own identity card within a minute would be duly rewarded for his effort. At the mention of a reward the students all became mobsters. They all leapt in unified disunity, screaming and clawing and fighting and hollering. As taught in their courses they were meant to be the most intellectual of all Homo sapiens, with their being in a school and learning what common men would not have had the privilege to learn. Yet, at this stage, they estranged the intellect from their character by extension of their conduct. They struggled, and were naught but 'Homo' at that point. For the entire world, they even bore semblance to the least intelligent, but most brutish of man's evolution phases – the Australopithecus Africanus; the early man. They reverted to their basic instinct, which informed them that survival belonged to the fittest. Man and woman were united in disunity.

After one full minute the professor commanded in a loud voice that the fray be ceased, and the bag brought to him. The poor bag had been sorely used in that one minute of intensive barbarism, and was looking very torn and haggard. He then asked that those who had seen their identity cards should move to the left, while those who had not should move to the right. Those who had found their identity cards did not number more than twelve, a good ten percent of the class, and they had smug looks on their faces, perhaps because they were of the opinion that the parabolic hour had come when the wheat would be separated from the tar, and the righteous would be rewarded while they who had conducted themselves less 'affabrously' would be cast into the lake of fire. The smug ones were eager to watch those who had not been so lucky burn, and they waited patiently for the professor's judgment. The professor then put the bag out to the unlucky band and asked one of the students to begin to give the identity cards to their various owners. In less than the same one minute it took the twelve smug fellows to acquire their identity cards, this new method ensured that about eighty of the remaining fellows obtained their cards.

The professor then called the twelve smug fellows to the scrutiny of the others and said all twelve of them were as guilty as the rest of them, for they had initially all participated in the struggle and were only unlucky not to have found their cards. It could have been any of them among the twelve. That kind of lifestyle, he elucidated, would help no one but the individual conducting himself so selfishly. He explained also that one of the reasons there were so many people on earth, and so many problems, is because people in their selfish haste to become successful have forgotten how to be humane. They are selfish and are trying to ensure they make it by all means. The twelve who had gotten their own identity cards all had torn clothes, disheveled hair, scratches on their skin and other such signs of struggle. Whereas, if they had simply two people distributing the identity cards, they would not have had any injuries at all and would have found their identity cards within a short period. By this time, all the students; smug lot and unlucky lot alike, were visibly wearing the hangdog look. With that, the lesson on helping was over.

The same is the case in Christendom. Many Christians think they have it all figured out; obtain salvation, maintain a pious life, and at the end of it all, go to Heaven. They have forgotten all about evangelism. Then there is another hypocritical lot that consists of those who are Christians only by word of mouth and not by the intents of the heart. They would divest themselves of the scarves and instead clad themselves in the *hijab*. They would tuck the Bible somewhere and instead sport a Qur'an. They have forgotten what the Lord says about one not being able to serve two masters, and what the Lord also said about how those who serve him must do so in truth and in spirit. In the book of Matthew 6:24 the Lord says; "No man can serve two masters: for either he will hate the one, and love the other; or else he will hold to the one, and despise the other. Ye cannot serve God and mammon." Also in the book of John 4:23-24, the Lord again says; "But the time is coming – indeed it's here now – when true worshipers will worship the Father in spirit and in truth. The Father is looking for those who will worship him that way. For God is Spirit, so those who worship him must worship in spirit and in truth."

So while some took this to heart, there were others who did not. Take the story of Abraham Akong, a Christian, and his wife Rachael Akong, formerly Alima Abdallah, who was born into a Muslim home. They had met and fallen in love while they were still studying. They had both attended the prestigious University of Johannesburg in South Africa, and while Abraham was studying accounting, Alima was his junior colleague. They always had that connection, that spark which is only borne out of true love, which was what endeared them to each other. They had started off as friends. He used to teach a few junior colleagues who were her classmates. He was very brilliant, of that there was no question. He taught them well. Then as Abraham and Alima got closer, they made their feelings known to each other.

By the time he completed his studies in South Africa, they had fallen uncontrollably and irrevocably in love with each other. The major question was what they would do about the love they had for each other. Abraham had been on a scholarship, and he already had employment waiting for him in Sudan. It was his Church Diocese headed in Ethiopia that had sponsored his education. He had been an orphan since the age of five. Alima on the other hand was two years his junior in academics, but she was twenty one which made her four years younger than he is. She was also from a very rich family. Her father was a rich merchant and a devout Muslim. He had eight children, of which Alima was the only girl, and the penultimate child. She had a younger brother with whom she was closest named Idris. He was nineteen years of age and very eager to please his brothers so that he could prove he was ready for anything the 'big boys' were ready for. He really did not like being viewed as the baby of the house, so he was trying to grow faster than his age.

Abraham and Alima agreed that he would go to Sudan to start a life, while she would complete her education then join him in Sudan, and they would figure out how to further their relationship. At the completion of her studies in South Africa, she returned to Sudan. They rekindled the flames of their love affair, by which time her father had started telling her to marry his Muslim friend's son, Bashir Ahmed. This prompted Abraham Akong, who was also financially stable, to act fast. Alongside Alima, they went to visit her parents where he asked for her hand in marriage. Her father did not say anything, but simply walked out on them. Her brothers followed suit. Idris, who genuinely wanted to know his sister's boyfriend but did not want to seem sissyish, walked up to Abraham, shook his hand, and also left. Her mother was the only one who sat both of them down and advised them strongly not to pursue the route of madness which they were plying. She reminded her of the kind of person she knew her father to be: a man who would never allow his daughter to marry a Christian man. She also advised Abraham that if he really loved Alima as his courage to walk up to her parents seemed to prove, he would do what was best for her, and let her go and marry a Muslim man. He would forget about her and go on with his life. They pretended to understand, but secretly plotted their way forward. Her father meanwhile, called her one day and had a lengthy conversation with her in which he chided her very much for her thoughtlessness and promised he would forgive her misdemeanor if she would marry Bashir Ahmed. She did not reply immediately, and her father said he would consider any man she brought if he was a better option than Bashir Ahmed.

She knew she did not love Bashir Ahmed. The thought of him alone made her miserable. She pitied him because he was a womanizer and a spoilt child. He used his father's money to oppress people, as his father was one of the political office holders. On top of that, he was fifteen years older than she and very obese. Even though Abraham was not as financially buoyant as Bashir, he at least knew the value of money and was stable enough to take good care of her. He was not a pompous man; and he was a moderate five years her senior. Her stay in South Africa had westernized her a bit and she also knew the place of love in a relationship. Most importantly, she had fallen in love with Christianity and was beginning to love its ways and practices. She had converted to Christianity when she was in South Africa, and had gotten baptized and took the name Rachael. There was no way she was going back to Islam. All this while, she had been trying to hide it from her parents. She knew the time would come when they would have to come out with it, but with the way things were looking, there was no way she was going to reveal her true religion to anyone in her family.

She and Abraham knew they had to act fast. They decided to elope. They went to the court and got married the following week, planning to elope in Kenya in the upcoming month. Her name on the marriage certificate was Rachael Akong. Alas, in the words of William Shakespeare, "The course of true love ne'er did run smooth." On the day they were wedded, among the other families that were getting wedded at the court was the family of one of her father's business associates. The man called her father to enquire why he did not get a marriage invitation, and why he was not present at the wedding.

Her father was, of course very lost and by the time he was able to establish what his daughter was doing, he and his seven sons went to the court. By the time they arrived, his daughter and her husband were gone. Alima had not told anyone where she would be. It was common practice for her not to go home sometimes for two days in a row because of her work. All she would do was send her mother a text message that she would not be sleeping at home, and they would not expect her. On this day, she had also sent a message to her mother again telling her she would not be home. However, Alima's father informed her mother that 'her' daughter had gone and disgraced the family by getting married without their knowledge or consent to a Christian man. She was shocked.

Her father ended the call and went into the court to enquire and obtain information about what was happening, and who it was that his daughter had married. He also wanted to know where the man stayed. Usually, it was not court rules to divulge such sensitive information, but with sufficient financial encouragement, the marriage registrar decided to look the other way while one of Alima's brothers sifted through the marriage book. He got the information that they needed and they all trooped over to Abraham's house. They went there and knocked on the door. By this time, it was around four o'clock in the evening. A voice from inside asked who was there, and one of the sons answered very politely that he came from the community development council, and that he wanted to see Abraham Akong. As soon as he opened, they pushed their way inside. It was a three bedroom flat, and they immediately started beating him, asking where their sister was. Alima stepped out of the kitchen where she had been cooking. It was the noise that attracted her because she really did not know who was there. Upon seeing her family, the napkin she was holding fell from her hands. The sight of her new husband on the floor and her brothers trouncing him filled her with so much fear. She was apprehended and made to watch. Then both of them were shot in the stomach and left to die. Neighbors heard the gunshots and called for the police. By then, her family had gone and the police only met her breathing faintly. They rescued her just before she lost too much blood. It was much later that she was able to recount what happened to the police. She did not divulge the full extentof what happened though because she was scared she would be sued afresh. She only said it was the work of assassins and that they wore balaclavas so she could not identify them.

Abraham died for the God he believed in, and even though death came to him suddenly and unexpectedly, this did not mean he was not prepared for it. He was a man of principles; he lived all his life like he would die the very next minute, so he always tried to stay within the sheltering fence of both redemption and salvation. He always lived a pious and sanctified life.

Upon the lives of those willing to sacrifice, comes the favor of God. He shows his power in extraordinary ways for those who give their lives for the Kingdom.

The Ministry of the Smiths

The Smiths are only one example of the many nice people who are trying to help the citizens of Sudan in a humanitarian way. Quite a while ago, they were interviewed by The Blaze, a website that focuses on stories of persecution of Christians.

The road hasn't been an easy one for the Smiths, as Kimberly, a missionary to Sudan, – who frequently jumps through hoops and smuggles herself over the border in an effort to reach the orphanages she runs in Sudan – was attacked and raped by a group of Darfurian refugees on one of her trips to the region about ten years ago. It was a horrific experience that she's still working through, but it hasn't dissuaded her from going back to Sudan and South Sudan again and again – all in an effort to help the poor, lost and downtrodden.

Now, Smith is using her tragic story to help other women who have experienced similar horrors.

"I have not overcome it. I still move through it. It's a part of my story now; it's a part of me. So how do I learn to live with that? And how I am learning to live with it by being willing to just continue in that sorrow, and see what God wants to do with it."

At first, Smith said she lived in denial until she was able to process what unfolded. Eventually though, she began working through her emotions surrounding the life-changing event.

One of the ministry complications Smith has is that her husband, Milton, is an insulin-dependent diabetic who is unable to accompany her into Sudan. While he struggles with her going into the danger zone without him, she said he blesses the decision, as they both feel called to help the orphans there.

"He does a lot of discipleship with our indigenous leaders. So it is a huge sacrifice for him but he sees the difference in his calling versus my calling, and he blesses my calling," Smith said. "It doesn't mean he's okay with it, and he is on his knees a lot having to continue to surrender each and every time I go back."

Despite their struggles and the immense pain they've experienced, Smith said their hard work has paid off.

"Fast forward ten years, and now we have three orphanages, one in the Nuba Mountains of Sudan, one on the border of Darfur, and one in Southern Sudan down near the border of Uganda," Smith said, adding that her ministry has also launched the region's first high school.

Rather than a seamless process where she has felt as though God has given her a neatly wrapped game plan,

Smith said that launching and running Make Way Partners has been a long and grueling process, logistically speaking.

Take for instance, the barriers she faced in organizing and building the orphanages.

"All of the building supplies had to be brought in … we had to bring them 2,000 miles, from Nairobi with no roads and no bridges. It was hostile terrain the whole way," she said. "Everybody said, 'don't do it, and don't do it Kimberly, if you do, it will kill your ministry.' "

But she recalled her husband saying that they didn't need to be afraid and that they simply needed to be faithful, so they forged on.

She also explained how difficult it is to get into Sudan, noting that no commercial airlines fly in and that she cannot get a visa to enter the country.

"They won't legally let me in, so I have to smuggle myself across the border from the south into the north," There's also the impending threat that their hard work and dedication will be destroyed by bombs, as ongoing violence rages in the region.

"We're not naïve to think that God has promised that all of this won't be blown up," she said. "It might, but I think that what gives us the courage, the faith to move forward in these difficult times is because we know that's not where our promise is, that's not what our hope is.

Smith said that the journey into Sudan began when she and her husband served as missionaries in the Iberian Peninsula more than tenyears ago, where they noticed that a local Portuguese brothel was filled with African immigrant children.

"The youngest was six, the oldest was about sixteen, and the thing that was the most shocking to me is it was almost half and half boys and girls," she said. "It wasn't all just little girls."

Smith said it was a six-year-old boy who initially told her in 2003 about the horrific things that were happening to him and the other children – a revelation that launched Smith and her husband into combating human trafficking head-on.

"We had one little boy that we were able to get medical documentation on the one that came and showed me what was happening ... – it was obvious he was being sodomized, he was very physically traumatized, cut, torn, and bloody and so it was a clear case with him," Smith explained.

She said that the little boy was taken to a hospital where a medical record was taken, but that the brothel's owners were tipped off, leading to a long and painful legal battle.

Forced to take legal avenues to try and gain access to other children being abused in the brothel, Smith said that she and her husband had to send their own children back to Alabama to stay with friends and family following threats from the brothel owner that he would take her daughters. This was all uncharted territory for Smith, who said she didn't know much about human trafficking at the time. It took two years to shut down the brothel, as Smith and her husband sat on police office and courthouse steps until authorities – whom she said were complicit in the problem – listened to their pleas.

"We spent days just trying to get someone who would even open their door and listen to what was happening," she said. "But we'd already had this one child taken away so they knew they were about to be exposed and they just clamped down and refused to see us."

But rather than back down, Smith said she called the International Justice Mission, a human rights group that helped guide her and her husband through the process.

"They said this is the one time that you do want to be the ugly American, no matter what; you don't leave, you refuse to look away because it will only be from external pressure –

that and exposure —that this will begin to change," she recalled the organization telling her. "And they were right, but ... the [brothel owner] threatened to kill us. It was a very just horrifying time."

Afterward, she said that she and her husband felt a "deep...call to go where these children and women were being taken from and try to work to stop it from happening at the root cause."

In the end, Smith said the victory was "bittersweet." While she and her husband ended up ensuring the brothel was closed, she said that none of the children were given any after-care.

"The Portuguese government just literally swept it under the rug and ended up sending them back to the shanty-towns where they had come from as illegal immigrants because they were all from Africa," she said. "They were illegal, they had no documentation."

Smith said that these kids might have ended up getting trapped again in the same system from which she had rescued them.

"The government just sends them back to the shanty-town, where they had come from — been taken from to begin with — which means they were going to just be recycled through the whole process," she said, with a look of sadness.

Smith said that she and her husband began to look at ways that they could curb the problem at its source. They began studying the problem and quickly realized that some of the worst places where human trafficking unfolds are locations where there's been active war or a weak government.

Soon they found themselves in Moldova and Romania, working with children there, but a ministry peer kept saying that if they really wanted to help the children in the direst situations that they should go to Sudan – something Smith said she initially rejected.

"I was scared to death; I had never been in a war zone before. I hadn't been one of those kids that thought, 'Oh when I grow up I'm going to be a missionary in Africa;' none of that was on my radar screen and so I spent a lot of time on my knees and with my friend encouraging me from Voice of the Martyrs to go before I finally agreed to go."

Considering her husband's condition, Smith went to Sudan alone to scope out the situation and what she observed there she summarized in one pointed word: "devastation."

"Miles and miles and miles and miles of nothing except trees blown up where bombs had been dropped ... villages burned to the ground," she said. She saw babies emaciated, who could barely stand up, walking around naked. "I'll be walking through a field and pick up one shoe, you know, one little, like a sandal flip-flop sort of thing from a child and right next to shells, bomb shells, bullet shells, bullet casings and bones."

Despite her deep desire to help the afflicted and despite the horrific sights she was observing, Smith admitted she was so afraid that she found herself counting the days until she could leave.

"Honestly, what I was doing is pulling out my calendar every day, checking that day off and saying thank God, I only now have ten more days, or thank God I only have nine more days, and then I can go back, and I will have done what I need to do," she said. "I even thought, 'You know, I'll write a book about it. I'll inform people and then I'll be off the hook."

But Smith said that God had very different plans for her. She met a Sudanese man named James Lual Atak at one of her last stops on the border of Darfur. As a former lost boy, he abandoned an opportunity to move to the U.S. so that he could stay behind and help orphans in need.

With few resources, he worked with what he had in an attempt to educate young people and to assist them in learning valuable educational and life skills.

"He had no money, he had no resources, and when I found him all he had were three chalk boards ... propped up against mahogany trees out in the Sahara desert," Smith said.

At the time she remembered thinking, "What is he doing?" as she saw him bouncing around from group to group, reciting numbers and the ABCs in an effort to educate children whom she said were clearly suffering from malnutrition and starvation.

After staying with him for a few weeks, Smith decided to leave him $5,000 in an effort to help him get food and resources for the children. When she left, she said she felt as though her work was done – but she was wrong.

Despite having no running water or electricity, he had a satellite phone and, once Smith was home, he began calling her with positive updates about the children and about the suggestions Smith had given him that he was implementing.

Though she was skeptical, Smith decided to return one more time a few months later – and she was stunned by what she observed. The kids were eating and looking healthier and he had made additional progress in noteworthy areas.

It was at that moment that she realized she'd be much more involved in Sudan than she ever thought, partnering with the man to launch her first indigenous orphanage site. The number of children there has grown from just over 50 to well over 700.

Initially, Smith planned to simply offer food and education programs, but after hundreds of children died as aresult of not having viable living quarters, she launched full-scale orphanages – operations that continue to sustain lives.

While her reasons for going back and continuing her work are admittedly "complicated," Smith said that she feels "called and compelled" by God. She said that she hopes her story will help others recognize that, although there is immense darkness, there still is a lot that people can do to make positive change.

"You can support a child in a war zone; that is raising a generation of peace makers, not just foreign peacekeepers, but indigenous leaders that will change that nation one day," she said.

This inspiring story shows that God has not forgotten the people of Sudan. He sends those who will help them in their darkest hour of most dire need. There just may be times when the devil stirs up or militates his forces to prevent the people of Sudan from receiving answers to their prayers. Countless times these challenges are presented before Christians. As a result, it strengthens their faith and multiplies their angelic ministrations. The more challenges a Christian overcomes, the more angels the Lord assigns to him for his ministry. Therefore, as a Christian, it is required that we frequently encounter challenges. Whenever we are not facing a challenge, it is appropriate to dedicate ourselves to meditation on the word. This meditation is how the Lord arms his children with the necessary tools to overcome the next challenge.

CHAPTER 8:

THE PAIN AND SCARS

Of things past, the pain and scars still linger
in them to lofty heights I climb higher
we are sons of Cush, let no man harm us;
for we bear in us, the marks of Jesus.

Le Corbeau

There is a saying that 'what will not kill you will make you stronger.' Many disregard this axiom; I was once an ardent disregarder of this axiom too. Prior to my going to Sudan, I would vociferously engage anyone I saw propagating what I had always called this fallacious philosophy in civil discourse with the ultimate aim of relieving the person from the folly of this axiom. It was my school of thought in that age of brazen ignorance, you see, that what would not kill you would leave you so scarred, and so traumatized as to install either a proper phobia in you or to leave you with such a morbid hate for the thing in question that you will be substantially weakened from it, and thus would become less of the person you erstwhile were. There! That was my grand master-argument and I was of the opinion that it was a jolly good one too. I gloried uncontrollably in it. I got quite an impressive number of converts including some four members of the academia. I may have lived and died a self-conceited ignoramus, disseminating this torpid argument, if I had not heard of positive outcome from those who were determined to overcome. These stories must be told.

The Scottsdale Community College even shares the extraordinary story of Awout Bagat who went through a lot but has overcome her trauma to become one of the most hardworking and assiduous students in her class. Awout Bagat has a personal story of overcoming long odds to pursue a college degree – kidnapped at age ten, only to escape four years later and flee the country.

Even with this unimaginable background, Bagat considers herself fortunate to be where she is in life. At age thirty, she is married and has six children and is pursuing her dream of becoming a nurse.

"When I came to America, I worked two to three jobs to take care of myself, my mom and my siblings," Bagat said. "I moved to Arizona because the climate is good, but I didn't speak English, so I worked jobs like hotel housekeeping while I learned the language. I met a Sudanese man here and we married and made the decision to have our babies first, before I started school."

Bagat said she kept finding excuses for not going to school but, when she calculated all of the time she spent NOT in school, she was shocked that 11 years had gone by.

"I said 'no more.' I want to be an educated mother and be an example for my children. It's not easy for a mother working full time and going to school. Sometimes I don't sleep, but I can't tell my children to go to school if I don't go."

Bagat is completing her nursing prerequisites and next semester will take the state exam required to enter the SCC/NAU RN to BSN program.

"Awout is my hardest working student," said English Faculty Matthew Healy. "She had her baby during the semester and still is getting an A in my class...she doesn't make excuses, but it's definitely not easy for her."

Healy could see her struggle but he and other instructors encouraged her to keep going.

"There was a time I thought it was too much, especially after I had the baby," Bagat said. "But, Mr. Healy kept telling me how good I am in his class and told me not to give up. He said, 'I'll make sure you get your degree,' and that motivated me the most. He wants me to get my education."

Bagat uses all of the academic support services available to her at SCC. "I grab all of the tutoring opportunities I can," she said. "If I have free time, I spend it on tutoring, especially during the day. Sometimes, I'm there at 6.00 a.m. waiting for the writing centre to open...I'm always exhausted, but it won't happen unless I put in the effort."

Bagat doesn't spend her valuable time regretting the past, but does encourage others to go to school while you're young. "I think about the four years before I had children and how I could have gone to school then and had a better paying job so much sooner," she said. "I encourage a lot of mothers to go to school and be an example for their children. You'll never find the time unless you make time, I tell them."

The incredible stories of those who have overcome are being spread through Christian circles and are encouraging those who have put their faith in trust in God.

Senior writer for the humanitarian agency, Church World Service, Chris Herlinger, whose real name is Sister Cathy Arata was writing for the National Catholic Reporter, and she shared another wonderful story of Father Rocha who left his home in Brazil to help those recovering from trauma. The pain and helplessness the Sudanese people feel is apparently reaching many humanitarian agencies around the world. Father Raimundo Rocha is a Brazilian Comboni missionary since 2010 who spoke to her about his experiences in the Malakal diocese. Rocha, who had participated in the trauma workshop, was cautious about the peace agreement, saying there was widespread feeling in Juba that the warring factions weren't really committed to it.

Rocha had every reason to be cautious. In a remarkable first-person account of his own experiences, published in the *South Africa Comboni Missionaries' Worldwide magazine*, he told how in late January, he and others fled from the mission in Leer, located in the oil-rich area of Unity State. Threats from rebel groups and armed civilians wanting the mission's vehicles became increasingly dire, as did worries that Darfur mercenaries working alongside government troops might not "respect any church personnel. They would attack, destroy and even kill," he wrote. "We felt insecure, vulnerable and unprotected. This situation obliged us to leave the mission. It was a hard decision. We left."

But after arriving at a new locale, the mercenaries "came through the bush and attacked our group. They came shooting at us. We could hear the sound of bullets flying above our heads as we ran into the bush. The group was scattered and we had lost contact with one another. Each one thought everyone else would have died. Thanks be to God nobody was injured," he wrote.

"We regrouped in complete exhaustion as night fell. There is no doubt, if we were still alive, it was because God worked a miracle that day. There was fear, but no despair. We strongly felt God's presence."

When I spoke to Rocha, he repeated that theme. "I never felt as protected by God as I did in those moments," he said, and recounted the events calmly. But he became understandably emotional a few times, reflecting about the work that had gone into building the diocese's resources – schools and church buildings – and then to have them looted and destroyed.

"The town is practically destroyed, burned to the ground. He paused. "It's difficult, it's difficult. It's one of the toughest experiences of my life."

Of greater concern was that the Catholic community of Nuer people, including catechists, were dispersed "in the bush," seemingly safe, according to recent reports, but still facing a very basic dilemma: They're hungry, and are facing "an enormous lack of food security." Those in displacement camps at least had food and water. For those wandering, they were at risk. "In general, there's no food for these people: Markets are looted and people are still in the bush," Rocha said.

"We are looking for strength in God's grace. Only God's grace can help us overcome these ill feelings," Rocha said, about the difficulty in forgiving those who tried to kill him and his colleagues. "Our human strength is not enough. We are human beings; we feel weak; we feel traumatized. The feeling for revenge – it's real. It takes time. I don't know how long, but it takes time. It's a process and it requires a lot of prayer."

In the weeks following the trauma workshop, some working in the Malakal diocese tried to return, but the situation, Rocha said, "remained unsettled." Before the peace accord was signed, new violence flared up again during Holy Week, scuttling changes for a quick return back to Malakal.

A few got back, but most remained in the capital city. Rocha, for example, celebrated Easter at one of the United Nation's displacement camps in Juba. It was not yet "safe for a return to the diocese very soon," he said, and complicating things is the onset of the rainy season. "I just do not know when it will be possible," he added.

This did not surprise Mojwok, who did return briefly to Malakal but then returned to Juba. He said the peace accord remained fragile and that the two sides were still far, far apart. "The international communities have to make more efforts to help us," he said.

As for himself, after visiting family in Brazil, Rocha returned to South Sudan and is now the justice and peace ministry coordinator for the Combonis. In that capacity, he returned to Leer in October.

"It was very good to be able to re-visit Leer after the ordeal we went through. I was very happy to meet our people again and sad to learn that some of our parishioners lost their lives," he wrote. "Some died of hunger."

Rocha ended on a cautiously optimistic note: The Comboni missionaries have resumed their work in Leer, he told me. "Of course," he wrote, "we want to believe and hope for peace and the end of this conflict and people's suffering."

The thing about being good is that good is inherent in people regardless of their Christianity or their being of other religious faiths. There is in the Bible, the story of Cornelius who was so good, the Lord had to send Simon Peter to minister to him. Again, we find in Sudan, the inspiring story of a woman who rescues traumatized people and prevents grave injustice from bedeviling them. This is her story.

Magdalena Ehisa Tito, an elegant and extremely polite woman welcomed us into her home. The fifty-two-year-old, the only traditional chief in the whole of South Sudan, has become a role model for the women of Torit, Eastern Equatoria State. Chief Magdalena was born on November 25, 1959 in Torit. She went to primary school at the age of ten. She started work in 1977 as a veterinary assistant to the current Minister of Agriculture, Betty Ogwaro. At the age of nineteen, Tito got married, much later than most of her peers. At the time most girls were married off by the age of twelve.

Her marriage was not one many people would relate to today. Magdalena was first abducted and the abduction led into a marriage as was the practice at that time. "In our tradition when a man likes a woman, he will steal her either on her way to school or while going to fetch firewood. Once this is done, the family of the girl is informed and the marriage is arranged," Magdalena explained.

Even today early marriage remains a challenge for girls in post conflict South Sudan, preventing their enrolment, retention and completion of their education.

Magdalena had two sons but later divorced when her husband failed to pay the bride price of just one cattle to her family. The divorce was solely on the basis of non-payment of dowry and Tito received her divorce papers in 1983.

Her desire to serve her community moved Chief Magdalena to join the police in 1992 where she graduated in 1996. Thereafter, the police authorities sent her to train as a midwife. She said she was motivated to join the force because she wanted to contribute to keeping law and order in the south of Sudan. Though the training in the police college was tough, Magdalena was fit enough to carry out all the training schemes. It was during her time at the police training that the Khartoum government of Sudan changed the education curriculum from English to Arabic.

Chief Magdalena says this move came together with a series of other policies that made life difficult for the people of Southern Sudan, including the children, who had to automatically convert to learning in a new language. Chief Magdalena took part in the struggle for South Sudanese independence. She narrates stories of how she worked alongside other members of the Southern Sudan liberation movement to smuggle children to East Africa countries where they could study in English in defiance of the 'Arabization' of South Sudanese people.

Her contribution led to Sudan People's liberation Movement (SPLM) to recognize her as a leader for her community. True to their promise, when time came to nominate a Traditional Chief in Torit, she was nominated with other men. The Traditional Chiefdoms are male dominated and Magdalena wasn't sure she would be accepted. But she won the election in 2004 and became the first female traditional Chief in South Sudan. Many recognized her community service and in 2008, Magdalena was elected the Paramount Chief, leading 396 male chiefs in Eastern Equatoria State.

Chief Magdalena explained that culture and tradition are not favorable to women. "Traditionally, men and boys provide security for the animals (mostly cattle), while women perform domestic work such as providing food, cultivating, building houses and taking care of the children," she says. "Despite the huge responsibility the women have no say at home, including making a choice of a husband."

Chief Magdalena says this has led to many failed marriages and most times men abandon their wives and take on several other women, leaving a huge burden for women in terms of raising children. Chief Magdalena notes that this abandonment has led to some women resorting to alcoholism. She also says many women suffer domestic violence at the hands of their husbands and in-laws..

After the war, Chief Magdalena says, men returned and found the women had taken up some of their roles. "The men became lazy, most times they go out drinking and only return at night," she narrated, "Those men who are employed are not very different from the unemployed; most of them don't bring their salaries home for their families."

The inability of men to take up their responsibilities has increased gender-based violence in the communities. Women in polygamous relationships suffer a lot of neglect from their spouse, and sometimes they seek solace in the hands of other men, most times this results in arrest of such women.

Some of these cases make it to the chiefs in the area. Magdalena explains that most local Chiefs don't understand, or they do but fail to question the underlining cause and continue to sentence the women to spend six months in prison, while the men are left free.

The trauma from the long civil conflict resulted has been reflected in high levels of alcohol consumption among both women and men, leading to couples abandoning household care. Also men here can easily divorce their wives for irresponsible behavior with support from the traditional institutions.

As a woman, Chief Magdalena counsels women to avoid drinking and be role models for their children and the youths. She believes the woman has the responsibility of keeping the family together and imparting good morals to the children and the community at large.

In the cases where men have abandoned their wives, Magdalena advocates for such women to be compensated instead of being left to suffer alone to take care of the children and the household needs. Even though the war is gone, most women of South Sudan still face the culture war that limits the engagement of women in public spaces as well the culture that doesn't question and address violence against women.

For many women, the war trauma and continued marginalization and violence make it difficult for recovery even in the new independent state. The absence of central government and state programs means most timesdelivery of justice is shouldered by traditional leaders who often support men. In Torit there is no single counseling center for women and others who require psychosocial support. Magdalena calls on the Government of the Republic of South Sudan to ensure trauma healing is a component of the post conflict reconstruction process and also ensure rule of law and justice is brought to the ordinary citizens especially women.

The Sudanese are a strong people; however, their experiences have rendered them victims of various traumas, and left those needing help from people and organizations around the world. What many of them have faced and are recovering from might have been the end and perdition of some other nations.

CHAPTER 9:

LORD, WHEN DID WE SEE YOU?

In the dark hour of Osiris' grim doom
Lord have mercy on my soul let me bloom
In Hell's fiery fort, let me have no room
Thank you Lord, I can see Heaven's
Gates loom.

Le Corbeau

Pastor Matthew

When Pastor Matthew headed to Mading in Bor, South Sudan, he did not know what to expect, and he really did not try to expect anything. He maintained an epigrammatically stoic philosophy: "blessed are they who expect not, for they shall not be disappointed." As a matter of fact, this philosophy had served him well for countless times, so he had no plans to proselytize anytime soon. He knew how to hope, though. Without hope, he would have no faith, and without faith, what sort of Christianity would he be preaching? For the book of Hebrews in the Bible, as written by the Apostle Paul while he was under inspiration from God and was in the Spirit, instructed that, "Now faith is the substance of things hoped for, the evidence of things not seen." He therefore knew enough to hope, but not recklessly so.

Pastor Matthew had heard of the rich history of Mading, including that nearby, in Malek, just south of Bor, was where the first modern Christian mission in what is now called South Sudan was established. The late Archdeacon, Archibald Shaw was responsible for its establishment, and before long, Bor became the first area to host a Church Missionary Society station. The Islamists who had been converting everything from pillar to post across Sudan had been unable to reach that far south in their "Arabization" spree. Instead, they had come with Jihadist intentions and had persecuted the Christians soundly.

Pastor Matthew had also heard of the more recent history of the town, a certain massacre with deeply political footing as well as religious undertones, in which about two thousand people had been slaughtered. In addition, another twenty thousand had been displaced and were condemned to live in wretch and gloomy doom away from their homes, their lands, the people they loved, the sights they longed to see and the air they once breathed. These would survive, if they did, as aliens and outcasts; uncanny renegades that had been created by the merciless spirits of death, war, anarchy, and rage.

An air of grief continued to pervade the daily conduct and interactions of the people. Father Matthew also knew that despite their grief, chances were that he would be given a warm welcome upon his arrival, the sort that would ease his settling into the town. The more logical part of his reasoning reminded that he would probably meet with some hostility and would have to work his way into the people's hearts. The Sudanese had always been receptive to Christianity. For some reason, they had an inexplicable love for God. It was almost like a magnetic pull of sorts toward the Lord and his ways.

Pastor Matthew had been sent there not knowing a soul, but as the apostles of old had evangelized, he was to go there and try to evangelize the people. One major difference was that he was not planning to dust off his sandals and leave the town without converting a single soul for the Lord. Even though the war had all but estranged Christianity from these parts, he knew that there were still a few dying embers that could be fanned till they blazed brightly enough to feed the fire of the Lord. These would burn brightly and serve as a beacon to all who were lost and in need of hope. As far as lost souls were concerned, he was sure he would find them in abundant quantity at Bor. All he had to do was map out a strategy for winning them to Christ.

In this case, his strategy was to win over the local ruler and obtain a plot or two of land to establish a church which would also serve as a school where he could train the children. By doing this he would win over the parents and slowly lead the town to salvation in Christ. Meanwhile, Father Matthew was thinking about renting a building that was big enough to start a church in. He expected it would also serve a shelter over his head for the night until he could generate enough resources to make things better.

The bus dropped Father Matthew at the central bus stop in Mading and he took a look around. The town did not look too busy; at the same time it did not look overly idle either. It seemed an inconspicuous blend of busy and mellow life. The people did not appear hostile, although he received a few strange glances because of his cassock. (As far as looks go, Pastor Matthew's were not bad. He was still in his forties and was quite handsome. He was apparently not entirely South Sudanese because he had an Arabic look about him that made him look like he descended from the Cushites or Nubian Sudanese. He was tall and well-built because he did not take his exercises lightly. He would not be easily intimidated; in fact, his was a physique that would easily intimidate others, were he so inclined.) Generally however, a friendly aura pervaded the place. His spirit seemed to be telling him that everything was alright, so he quickly said a short prayer of thanks to God.

As he took stock of the environment, Father Matthew realized an eatery stood just across the road; it appeared to be the best place to air his inquiries, so he headed that direction. The street was quite dusty and the weather was sunny. In fact, the sweltering heat seemed to beat down on him without mercy, until he was strongly tempted to remove his collar, but he resisted the temptation and continued his steady pace. He entered the restaurant and found it was just half full. He said a silent prayer and walked straight to an empty table. The eatery was not much to look at – it was quite drab even and they did not have very acceptable hygiene, but he was not going to snub them.

The good Pastor had not sat at the table for five minutes before a waitress came to attend him, inquiring as to what he would like to eat. He requested a bottle of water and some chips. When all was set before him, Father Matthew called the waitress aside and asked if she knew of a reputable, decently priced hotel where he could spend the night. She told him that the town really did not have any grand hotels that would befit someone of his stature, but that his best bet was to stay at a motel. She told him about a good one just down the road from the restaurant.

As he was walking to the motel, he passed a graveyard and was quite interested to discover that many of the tombstones were cross-shaped and appeared to be Christian graves. He realized that many of these graves belonged to Christian martyrs. He added a mental note to not do anything that would cause himto join them.

True enough, before he had walked too far, the Pastor arrived at the motel. It was a dingy building with the sign hanging loosely from the first and only story. Matthew did not concern himself with the sight, however. Upon entering, he was met with the conspicuous absence of the receptionist. There was no one for him to talk to, but he strode to the counter anyway. It was only when he was standing up against the counter that he discovered the receptionist. Instead of sitting at her table, the woman was actually fast asleep on the floor behind it.

He cleared his throat loudly and the receptionist startled from her sleep, knocking her head on the wall in the process. Pastor Matthew turned his face from the embarrassing scenario, but he did not hesitate to speak. "Good evening. I'd like a room for the night, please."

The woman mumbled incoherently, but somewhere in the midst of her muttering the man was able to establish the motel rate. He paid her for a week. He collected the keys and went up to the room. On his way he heard the sounds of a lecherous couple indulging. The walls were thin, providing little hindrance to the reverberating sounds that filtered into the corridor. He shook his head. The world was fast debauching and there was nothing anyone was doing to stop it. That was why he was in the town; to evangelize the people and stop their moral famine. He did not want a repeat of Sodom and Gomorrah here. Every town riddled with licentiousness needed its Jonah. He knew this was one of the situations he was in the town to correct, and prayed that the Lord would grant him strength to do it. He got up to his room and thanked the Lord for journey mercies as well as the seemingly favorable situation. He knew it was the Lord's doing. He tidied the room to the best of his ability and made it habitable.

When he went down to get food and water some five hours later, he noticed the lecherous couple was now embroiled in the vituperative throes of a quarrel. It seemed like they were quarreling over how much the man was supposed to pay the woman for her permitting him to have her. He quickly said a prayer as he passed by their room without stopping to listen to the details of the argument. After eating, he lay down on the bed, said a prayer, and as he was about to sleep, the Spirit of God instructed him to go to the graveyard the next day. He was distraught, for he could not believe it. Did the Spirit not know of the deep hatred he had of being around anything dead?

That night he slept fitfully, waking intermittently because he kept having the most unsavory nightmares imaginable. He dreamed that moldy, rotten dead bodies surrounded him in a circle and were carrying out necrophilia orgies. His imagination seemed to be the chief agent of his undoing in this instance and he prayed against it. He did not like feeling weak so he intensified his prayers.

By the next morning, Pastor Matthew was resolute. He decided the best way to overcome this morbid fear – which he preferred to call a dislike – would be to actually face it. He would have to actually go to the graveyard and see what was in store for him there. He donned his black cassock complete with black socks and shoes. If he was going to the graveyard, he reasoned, he'd best look the part.

Grim as a judge, he strode to the place and entered. He began to look at the names on the tombstones and found that while the names were different, there was one portion of the graveyard where all the dates there were very similar. They all were marked around June, 1991. He even saw a mass grave containing only-God-knows-how-many dead people.

Conversation with a Gravedigger

As he was standing there struck by the horror of how so many people could have died at the same time, the gravedigger – who was also the cemetery custodian – came up behind him. Pastor Matthew had heard the man's soft footfalls, so he was not startled. He simply turned to face the man who only returned his searching gaze. They greeted each other and struck up a conversation.

Apparently, the man had been digging graves for twenty years and there was little to nothing he had not seen. What he rarely enjoyed however, was human company to talk to, so upon seeing Pastor Matthew clad in his cleric's garb, he knew he had found favorable company to talk to. Even the gravedigger was a Christian. Or better put, he had been a Christian, but not anymore. The lack of a church had made him backslide, and he had forsaken the assembly of the brethren. His favorite excuse was that there was really no assembly in the first place, so what was there to forsake? He licked his lips and began to talk non-stop about everything that seemed worthy of mentioning. It was during this conversation that the full details of what had happened were brought to his knowledge.

That gravedigger explained that during the early days when there was just one SPLRA, Christianity thrived in the town of Mading. The town benefited by its proximity to Bor, where Christianity was setting up a sort of stronghold in Southern Sudan. Evangelism was at its apex there and the going was really good. There were many evangelists spreading the gospel from Bor into South Sudan, ranging as far as the Nuba Mountains. Souls were being won for Christ.

But then the SPLRA-Nasir was formed and anarchy became the order of the day. In a bid to express their displeasure toward their former commander, the Nasir took to arms and attacked the people of Bor. Christianity and its evangelists were all subjected to mortal persecution.

Pastor Matthew was led from one grave to the other and the gravedigger, who seemed to have supervised the digging of most of the graves, told the story of how these great evangelists had died. Of all the stories, none interested Pastor Matthew more than the story of a certain Father Paul who arrived from Bor shortly after the first civil war in 1972. He had established the first church in Mading and preached a gospel of love, encouraging the people to accept Jesus Christ as their personal Lord and Savior. It was after they had accepted Jesus that he told them the implications of their actions on the Kingdom of God.

Strangely enough, the gravedigger remembered the Bible, both chapter and verse, that Father Paul had used when trying to emphasize that point. It was from the book of Matthew 25:34-40. Fortunately, Pastor Matthew had brought his Bible, and quickly navigated to the indicated Bible verse, *"Then the King will say to those on his right, 'Come, you who are blessed by my Father, inherit the Kingdom prepared for you from the creation of the world. For I was hungry, and you fed me. I was thirsty, and you gave me a drink. I was a stranger, and you invited me into your home. I was naked, and you gave me clothing. I was sick, and you cared for me. I was in prison, and you visited me.'" Then these righteous ones will reply, 'Lord, when did we ever see you hungry and feed you? Or thirsty and give you something to drink? Or a stranger and show you hospitality? Or naked and give you clothing? When did we ever see you sick or in prison and visit you?"And the King will say, 'I tell you the truth, when you did it to one of the least of these my brothers and sisters, you were doing it to me!'"*

Pastor Matthew read it over and over, relishing the impact these words would have had on a people who had been lost and were just recovering from the ravaging effects of war's harvesting sickle. According to the gravedigger, the effect of these lines was miraculous. Here was a God who was sympathetic to their situation and was extending to them a hand of love and friendship. This was very unlike their previous gods who were only vague figures of dread and would make them face the consequences of any misdemeanor. Their previous gods would wait to be called upon by way of sacrifice, which may have included a human life or two. Yet, despite their sacrifices, the gods would not necessarily respond. But, here was Father Paul preaching that; "Blessed *are* they which are persecuted for righteousness' sake: for theirs is the kingdom of heaven. Blessed are ye, when *men* shall revile you, and persecute *you,* and shall say all manner of evil against you falsely, for my sake."

The result was that when destruction finally came during the Bor Massacre of 1991, the Christian people of Mading, who were by this time very many, faced death with a bold heart and unafraid. For they knew a crown of righteousness awaited them in Heaven and viewed their death as God freeing them from the bonds of the flesh. They no longer feared; they knew they were the chosen of the Lord.

Pastor Matthew now knew why he had been called to Mading. The people needed their hopes revived; they needed the inner spark of their trust in Christ to be fanned until it became a blazing inferno that would consume the forces of evil and shine as a bright light to wipe away the darkness and restore the ways of the Lord in their lives. Pastor Matthew marveled at the miraculous ways in which God worked his wonders and knew that there was no way he could maintain his fear of death and the things pertaining to death. He knew God had sent him to the graveyard to be ministered unto by the unlikeliest of persons, a gravedigger. This ministration was crucial to Pastor Matthew's calling into the ministry.

Pastor Matthew listened intently as the gravedigger spoke, he had a wealth of knowledge. The gravedigger then recounted the story of Evangelist James Kat, a man who faced more recent persecution. Well after the secession, the Evangelist lived in Khartoum, Sudan. He was detained on a Tuesday morning by armed police who not only arrested him, but also dealt him several severe blows. They beat him thoroughly en route to the station, an unnecessary crime of battery in addition to harassment and violation of privacy. In a more judicially sound country this conduct would not have gone unpunished, but in Sudan, Evangelist Kat was lucky to avoid being shot in what the police would label as an act of self-defense. He had been detained for using the premises of the Evangelical Church of Sudan as his home.

There were many stories which the gravedigger recounted that day. He told Pastor Matthew of another Church leader who was duped out of his house by the government because they wanted to sell his land to a Muslim businessman. The injustice that people were suffering at the hands of their government simply because they do not subscribe to what the government's preferred religion was appalling. For this singular reason, many Christians have left the North and escaped into South Sudan where they can find considerable peace and the freedom to practice the religion they know and believe in. Ninety-five percent of the population in South Sudan is Christian. The people are not unjust to the Muslims in the area, yet the Muslims in the Northern Division are extremely hostile to the mention of Christianity. There is no better way to point out this injustice than by the judicial system they practice (and which they exploit for their own selfish religious gain) – sharia law.

Three years after Pastor Matthew arrived, well after he had fully settled in and the wave of Christianity was continuing to grow, he sent a message to the Church in Bor, asking the Senior Pastor to come to Mading to commission the new church unto the Lord. This tradition dates back to the times of the earliest church of the apostles. In the Bible, we find that they sent Peter and John to pray for the Samaritans after Phillip had done the major work of evangelizing them. It was after this that Phillip had an encounter with the Ethiopian eunuch. According to the book of the Acts of the Apostles, 8:14, "When the apostles in Jerusalem heard that the people of Samaria had accepted God's message, they sent Peter and John there.As soon as they arrived, they prayed for these new believers to receive the Holy Spirit. The Holy Spirit had not yet come upon any of them, for they had only been baptized in the name of the Lord Jesus. Then Peter and John laid their hands upon these believers, and they received the Holy Spirit." The senior Pastor met an organized congregation of over 5,000 Christians who worshipped at the new church Pastor Matthew had set up. He could do naught but weep for joy and give glory to the Lord.

CHAPTER 10:

THE POWER OF THE SPIRIT

The day draws nigh and the hour
is at hand When words once uttered
will be real as sand And to each man will
be judgment in kind For the word will
come again to this land.

Le Corbeau

The working of the Spirit has not yet failed to move men to perform extraordinary feats, both physical and spiritual. We have the account in the book of Judges where we see Samson, a judge over Israel, conquering the Philistines in a rousing victory. First, he fought a lion asunder. Then came unto him, the inspiration to compose a riddle with which he tasked thirty men of the Philistines, and when they had committed a great trickery (by which they persuaded his wife to coax the answer out of him) to acquire the answer, Samson was angered and he killed the Philistines who duped him. In many more instances, the Spirit of the Lord came mightily down upon Samson.

After he had completed many more slaughters of the Philistines, they finally wheedled the truth of his great power out of him – with the help of his wife, the traitorous Delilah – they cut off his connection to the Spirit of the Lord: his hair. Samson's bare head made it impossible for him to carry out the wondrous feats that had made him famous.

Some months later, the Philistines, inordinately pleased with their accomplishments (they had also blinded Samson), decided to make him a special guest of their mockery at a feast to their god and chief idol, Dagon. By this time, Samson was already re-growing his hair and – unbeknownst to his captors – was strengthening his connection to the Spirit of the Lord. That day, shortly after they had chained Samson to the pillars that supported the building where this great idolatry was being performed, he was once more, and for the final time, overcome by the Spirit. Armed with nothing but his bare hands, Samson pushed against the middle pillars that supported the building where they were worshipping their idol, breaking both pillars and bringing the entire structure down on his head. At his death, Samson killed over three thousand Philistines. This was more than the sum total of all the Philistines he had wiped out in his earlier life. All this, he was able to accomplish by virtue of the Holy Spirit descending upon him.

The Power of the Spirit – New Testament Style

We also have the account of the apostles on the day of Pentecost. They were gathered, by the Lord's instruction, in an upper room. There the Spirit of the Lord descended upon them and they spoke in other languages, as the Spirit gave them utterance, speaking tongues they had never learned before. The people in the town of Jerusalem (most of whom were devout Jews), were mystified by the strange speech, and could only ask if they were inebriated. Peter, emboldened by the Spirit, explained what they were witnessing by preaching soundly as the Spirit gave him utterance, and a whopping three thousand souls were won for the Lord that day. In a single ministration orchestrated by the Spirit of the Lord, the fledgling Church exploded in size.

Even more inspiring is the account of the deacon Stephen who was stoned to death while he could see into Heaven, with Jesus Christ standing at the right hand side of God. According to the Book of the Acts of the Apostles, Stephen had been actively preaching the Gospel in Jerusalem. He was a man full of the Spirit. This was apparent when certain characters contrived to testify against him, and while Stephen was giving his defense, all who fixed their eyes upon him could see his face shining brightly like that of an angel.

As he was speaking and filled with the Spirit, the people, incensed as if possessed by a demon, rushed upon him with a loud cry. They bound Stephen, hands and feet, and drug him outside the town. There, they lay their garments at the feet of a young Saul (later to become the apostle Paul) and commenced to stone Stephen, hurling stone after stone upon him. Stephen, his eyes opened to see the Father and the Son in Heaven, appealed for the life of the very mob that was killing him. This love and bravery in the face of death can only be found when the Spirit dwells within a person. This is one of the reasons for the great sacrifice of the Lord Jesus that his death would serve as a permanent atonement for our sins. Because of Jesus' death, all we need to do is claim the salvation offered through him, and the Spirit of the Lord will descend to dwell within us, whether or not we cut our hair!

Joseph Diing Manute

Such was the case of Pastor Joseph Diing Manute, a priest in North Sudan. During the influx of Arabic tradition, when there was intense persecution of Christians in the area, he braved Sharia law and continued to evangelize. His travails are typical of the injustice the Christians currently face in South Sudan.

This was the kind of injustice Pastor Joseph Diing Manute was preaching against when he spoke that Sunday. He had encouraged the Christians to fight the good fight, for at the end of it all a crown of righteousness awaited them. The congregation was enraptured by the Word. It was pure Rhema, the sort of truth which causes the Holy Spirit to descend. It was almost like Apostle Paul delivering the message on Christian living in Romans 12 which contained the famous lines, "And so, dear brothers and sisters, I plead with you to give your bodies to God because of all he has done for you. Let them be a living and holy sacrifice – the kind he will find acceptable. This is truly the way to worship him." This was the air in the auditorium when he finished his sermon.

As he was stepping down from the pulpit, an usher moved close and whispered in his ear that the police were waiting outside to see him. He said he would be there in a minute because he wanted to pray, seeing as he had just finished a sermon. He knelt down and prayed, and the Lord showed him that the time was drawing near, so he had to be strong and be of good courage. He went out to meet the authorities. There were about ten men standing beside a vehicle that looked like a bullion van, popularly known as a "Black Maria." Two police cars served as escorts. One of the men brought out what appeared to be an arrest warrant and served it to Pastor Diing Manute, informing him that he was under arrest. Then the policeman produced a pair of handcuffs, intending to cuff the Pastor, when some members of the church reacted. They quickly approached the police officers and said there was no way they would arrest anyone.

Before Pastor Diing could even protest, he was in the middle of a physical altercation in the making. The church members outnumbered the police officers three to one, but the police officers were armed while the congregation wasn't.

The three police officers fired a volley of shots into the air and dragged the pastor into the Black Maria.

While this was going on, the church members quickly recovered from the shock of the gunshots, reinitiated their resistance against the arrest of the pastor. Then one of the policemen "forgot" to raise his gun in the air before shooting. Instead, the highly trained officer of the law somehow managed to leave his gun facing the oncoming crowd as he shot three times.

The shots resonated in the air. Two church members dropped without a sound, while a third fell, hollering his lungs out. A second policeman, and then a third and a fourth pointed their guns at the flummoxed crowd, and let loose a hail of bullets. The flabbergasted lot, released from their initial state of paralyzed shock, hightailed it out of the parking lot. The bodies dropped to the ground. The police stopped shooting and zoomed off. The press was agog with the news that policemen had carried out a massacre in the church. As a humanitarian crime it gained a lot of public attention. Around the world, people were demanding justice for the ill-treatment of this church.

The fate of the pastor was unknown, for he had been denied access to his Christian lawyer. Only after a heated rant on a TV show by a human rights activist, Tut Garang, was the pastor allowed to see any lawyer. He was charged with disturbing the peace, waging war against the state, and undermining the constitutional system. He could be facing anything from life imprisonment to death for the latter duo of charges that had been leveled against him.

As for the Christians who had died that day at the church, they were reported as trying to brew anarchy and attacking the policemen; the policemen only shot when their lives were in danger. That was the summary of the report released by the Ministry of Defense. There was no one alive to question it.

One day, much later, Pastor Joseph mounted the pulpit in Omdurman and began to preach. He started his sermon by quoting, "Blessed *are* they which are persecuted for righteousness' sake: for theirs is the kingdom of heaven. Blessed are ye, when *men* shall revile you, and persecute *you,* and shall say all manner of evil against you falsely, for my sake. Rejoice, and be exceeding glad: for great *is* your reward in heaven: for so persecuted they, the prophets which were before you." Then the pastor began to highlight how grave the injustice was that the Christians were suffering at the hands of the Arabic Muslims. He talked on for hours about how the Lord had warned them that their suffering was not the direct handiwork of the people who persecuted them, but rather the devil who was working in those people. He exhorted the church to wage war against the devil. He reminded the people that they wrestled, "not against flesh and blood, but against principalities, against powers, against the rulers of the darkness of this world, against spiritual wickedness in high places."

Prophet Matthew

The prophet had been preaching boldly to a decent crowd about how the ravaging sickle of war would visit the people of Sudan as prophesied by the prophet Isaiah. He had talked extensively about how – in the book of Isaiah 18 – the ancient prophet had prophesied about the people of Sudan being potentially destroyed if "swift messengers" did not go and go and warn them. He highlighted the evil treatment of the Arabic and Islamic majority against the Christian minority as one of the reasons the Sudanese people, who had always been fierce and warring, may never know peace.

This was not his first time delivering such a message. In fact, this had been his usual nomadic preachment. He had for years been traveling from town to town, spreading this very message to all who cared to hear. Unfortunately, it proved to be the last time he would preach such a message.

Matthew was still preaching when he was shot from within the crowd. Naturally, the whole crowd disappeared, but the pastor died even before his body had crashed to the ground. His eyes were still open, looking to the heavens, but his body was just an empty shell. The life had gone out of it.

The authorities, upon hearing of his death, did not make an immediate appearance. They arrived at the scene of the grievous crime a full hour later to commence their investigations. By this time, most of the initial crowd that had been there listening to his teachings had left. Only a few faithful, bent on assisting the police, stayed to wait all that time for their arrival.

The police arrived on the scene and carted away the body, they asked a few questions, and "commenced" investigations. Days ran into months, which ran into years. The people kept crying for justice, but the killer was never found.

Pastor Abraham Bior

One Reverend Father Abraham Bior, a Catholic priest, grew vociferous on a radio talk show after hearing the report and accused the government very vehemently of corruption. Two days later, a warrant for his arrest had also been issued, and the priest was imprisoned for the same crimes as Pastor Diing Manute.

The case dragged on and on, and lawyers tried to defend the two men's innocence. This was extremely difficult because the Sudanese government was highly displeased with the activities of both pastors. The case dragged on for a long time, and both pastors were eventually sentenced to death. The case was appealed and the pastors' offenses were revisited. After much debate, the judge concluded that the pastors were inciting the people to anarchy. The only condition under which they would be released was if each would sign an affidavit stating that they would never preach publicly again, but would instead maintain a low profile. They were given a week to think about their decision.

The pastors prayed long and hard about their situation. At the end of the week, they knew what to do. Both of them realized they had received a calling from the Lord and decided there was no man or law that would make them rescind their calling. They would preach on. They made this quite clear in the courtroom and the judge sentenced them both to death by hanging.

This case garnered a lot of public attention, but there was nothing that could be done about it. Both pastors were executed the following week, but by the way they comported themselves, they gained the respect of all who saw them. The two were very brave. They were unfazed by threats and were not swayed by the reality of impending death.

On a regular basis, pastors in Sudan face this kind of grim reality.

CHAPTER 11:

YOU DID NOT CHOOSE ME, BUT I CHOSE YOU

Ye did not choose me, but I chose you,
and appointed you,
that ye should go and bear fruit, and
that your fruit should abide:
that whatsoever ye shall ask of the Father
in my name, he may give it you.

John 15:16

Legends are not all made up. True, some of them are the aesthetically sound products of a bard's imagination, but some of them are simply overblown and exaggerated narratives of real events that developed over time. Some of these stories eventually die out, but some stand the test of time and are retold for years to come, even to the end of an age. This is where the distinction between real and made up is most obvious. What is real will remain real; it will stay within the bounds of reality.

The people of Sudan have seen the worst of reality, and they have seen the best of it. They have been at the top, and they have been down in the bottom. They have sought the face of the Lord and they have turned away from him. Wherever their story is told, it would seem like the stuff of legends, but the reality of it lies within. It is inherent in the pain and the sadness. How did a land that boasts of having produced some of the best rulers in the world – King Tirhakah, King Shebitku, or King Piye – sink so low that it is now riddled with strife?

Their story has become a beacon of hope to many Christians around the world. It is a common practice for people to tell others when they begin to moan and groan about the bleakness of their lives, that they should be thankful for their situation. If they heard of other peoples' misfortunes, they would see that their own quandary is a relatively mild one. They are reminded that some people would be glad to be in their shoes.

The people of Sudan are like a motivational book which, when one reads it, one is spurred on to accomplish greater things. Many of the Lost Boys and Girls of Sudan are far from home, having left what used to be their homeland in the most uncomfortable of situations. During their great migration across the desert, some of them were eaten by wild beasts, becoming nourishment for animals. They fed on leaves. They walked barefoot. They often had to drink their own urine to avoid dehydration. Despite how intriguing this sounds, one cannot begin to fathom the real extent of this misery unless one has experienced it first-hand. Those who made it out alive are the lucky ones. Mass rape, genocide, hunger starvation and famine are the lot of those who remained behind. When did displacement become a fortunate thing in human history?

Who can say that these people do not need companionship; that they do not need help? Who can say where their path will lead? For many, they have fallen from kings to slaves. They are slaves to a culture that is not theirs. They now pass their days in a land that has no real historic connection to their ancient culture. Many of the people of

Sudan are now Arabized and have become more Islamic, more Sunni than the Sheikhs of Arabia. They are taking to heart the culture of a land that they should instead be governing. If they could conquer the Egyptian kingdom of old, one wonders, how it is that they have now been made to stoop so low. "How art the mighty fallen!"

This grim reality has become such that wherever the story of the Sudan and the Church in the Sudan is told, lives are being changed. The phenomenal "Save Darfur" movement transcends the traditional realm of faith communities, motivating tens of thousands to stop the genocide. The mission of the Church in Sudan to the world is to be a catalyst in transforming and liberating lives that are bound up – often in privilege – to serve God as they live out their days in this world.

Lost Boys

The next few pages will focus on the real life stories of a few of the Lost Boys and Girls of Sudan. Many of these embattled children have immigrated to the United States and are becoming effective servants to the suffering Sudanese. They know firsthand what horrors their countrymen are enduring and they, too, have experienced the trauma of displacement.

My Story

On one early morning, my city, the city of Dong was attacked. During the attack on the city of Dong, I was at the cattle camp twelve to fifteen miles away from the attack. The villagers in Dong fled south once the attack started. My parents and family fled southward toward Uganda, a few thousand miles south. They were forced to flee in that direction as a result of this highly planed strategic attacked enacted by the government.

The next morning, the cattle camp was attacked. It was early in the morning when the attack begun. That morning, the other children and I were going among our daily business of attending the cattle. At this point in the morning, the cattle were still located within the camp. The cattle had yet to be taken out to the fields for grazing. Suddenly, we heard the sounds of helicopters gunships flying overhead of the cattle camps. Without any knowledge of the horrors that were about to occur momentarily, the other children and I got excited. We started jumping up and down with excitement of seeing these helicopters. Unfortunately, this excitement of seeing helicopters at our village lasted only momentarily. Immediately they began to fire upon the cattle camp. I remember the sounds of the guns firing from the helicopters and the first sight of cattle being shot and dropping all around the camp.

As soon as the shooting began, we realized immediately that our only chance of survival was to flee. The position the helicopters were firing from forced us to flee to the east, toward Ethiopia. As we began to flee south, the clouds of cattle from the camp began to follow us and there was nothing we could do about it. At this point the other children and I were now fleeing east toward Ethiopia, while my parents and the rest of my family from the city of Dong were fleeing south toward Uganda.

Into the Desert

We began to flee eastward across the desert. At this point, it was just the group of children from our village's cattle camp. As we would trek further eastward toward Ethiopia, we would eventually meet up with groups of other children from cattle camps in other villages that were attacked in the same method and on the same day that the city of Dong was attacked. But as for right now, it was just our cattle camp crossing the desert.

It took us three days to cross the desert. While crossing the desert, we had no food, no water, no clothing, and no appropriate equipment for crossing the desert. During this time crossing the desert, many children died from the extreme conditions. Other children would simply lose all strength and collapse, unable to continue fleeing. While crossing the desert, temperatures would rise to easily over 115 degrees Fahrenheit. We suffered from extreme dehydration as a result of this extreme heat and inadequate equipment to prepare for it. In extreme dehydration, many horrible things begin to occur. Your mouth becomes extremely dry. After having a dry mouth, it begins to become cracked, and will eventually bleed from the dryness. Your tongue will then become unable to move. Your eyes will become cracked, swollen, and then it becomes increasingly difficult to blink. Your stomach loses all feeling. Children who began to develop these symptoms of dehydration did not survive. To combat this extreme thirst from crossing the desert with no water, we were forced to drink our own urine to survive.

In addition to suffering from the extreme dehydration, we were also being pursued by the northern governmental forces that attacked the city of Dong. During the three days of crossing the desert, helicopters would patrol from time to time looking for us. The desert landscape contained many hills and areas of brush. During the day, we would hide amongst the slopes of the hillsides and brush to stay out of sight of any patrols looking for us. Once night arrived, it became cold and we would continue our trek east.

To Ethiopia

After we trekked three days through the desert, we continued onward for three months toward Ethiopia. As we approached Ethiopia, we had to spend one week crossing through a dense jungle. Similar to the geography surrounding the city of Dong, this region of South Sudan had no roads which would allow for easy passage through the jungle.

As we made our way through the one week trek through the jungle, we encountered more hardships. We began to suffer from animal attacks. While traveling through the jungle, friends of mine were attacked, taken, and killed by lions. Other children grew weary and gave up and stayed behind in the jungle.

We eventually made our way through the jungle and arrived at the Ethiopian border. The border between Ethiopia and South Sudan is geographically marked by the Gilo River. The Gilo River spans the border between Ethiopia and South Sudan, runs approximately 200 miles, had a depth up to 20 yards, and has a width ranging between 80 and 100 yards. The Gilo River is a river in Sudan that is famous for being heavily infested with crocodiles and other dangers animals.

Once we arrived at the Gilo River, we lived for a short time on the border of the two nations, between the jungle and the Gilo River. We stayed here while waiting for canoes and rafts to arrive to safely carry us across the river into Ethiopia. We waited for aid to come, but aid never arrived. As we waited by the river, no one even knew we were there. The closest cities were many days away. We ended up staying here on the border for two weeks. During these two weeks, we survived on wild fruits from trees.

One morning, two weeks after we were living on the edge of the river, a man from Kansas arrived. We never found out who this individual was, or what his exact business was for being at the Gilo River. We figured he was probably a missionary working in the area that happened to overhear crucial information broadcasted on a government radio channel. This man proceeded to warn us that the government knew our location and were going to launch another attack tomorrow morning. By this point, the children from our village met up with children from other villages, and we numbered close to 29,000 refugees, mostly children.

Having found out that we were going to be attacked once again tomorrow morning, we found some sticks to try to measure the depth of the water to see if we could find a way across the river. Unfortunately, the water was too deep to easily cross. Unable to easily cross the river, we ended up staying until the following morning. By late morning, soldiers from the government knew our location and began to shell our encampment with mortars. While we were being bombed, the government also deployed infantry into the nearby jungle to attempt to search for us. It did not take too long after the bombardments began for our turmoil to grow once more. We heard once more the familiar sound of helicopter gunships flying our direction. This time, we had between four and six helicopters above us.

Shortly after their arrival, the helicopters began to open gunfire and bombardment upon us. Everything instantaneously turned into complete and utter chaos. Smoke soon filled the entire encampment and you could not see where you were going. In the midst of the smoke, other children were being shot and dropping dead all around me. The next thing I remember is seeing some of the helicopters landing nearby. Once they landed, solders were disembarking from the helicopters and opening up machine gun fire upon us.

At this point we were faced with a choice. The first option was to remain where we were and be captured by the governmental solders from the north. This meant we would be forced into a life of slavery and brainwashing into Islamic ideology to become a terrorist. The alternative option was to run into the river and try to escape. A lot of children ran right into the river. Many of them could not swim and ended up drowning, while others were eaten by the crocodiles that infested the Gilo River. The solders continued to open fire upon children attempting to cross the river, killing many more who were attempting to swim across.

Both my cousin and I had some experience swimming. My cousin had more experience, so he ended up swimming across the river first. I followed close behind, holding onto his leg to help me get across. While crossing, we grabbed hold of water lilies, sticks, or any other objects we could grasp to help improve our chances of getting across the Gilo River alive. While swimming across the river, we were seeing everything through the eyes of fear. Although the river is only 80 to 100 yards across from Sudan to Ethiopia, the river felt as if it was five miles wide.

Arrival in Ethiopia

We eventually made it to the other side of the Gilo River alive. Once we made it across, the government soldiers from northern Sudan stopped firing and we were safe. We were lucky to be alive, especially considering a large number of other children were either killed or captured into slavery.

The other children and I continued to flee eastward into the Ethiopian jungle. We eventually came across some local villages located not too far from the Gilo River. Having no place to go, we were allowed to camp alongside these villages. We were now safer than we had been since we were at home in our villages in Sudan. While we lived in Ethiopia, we would form groups of twenty to thirty children and construct small houses to live in. In the mornings, we would journey outward into the jungles to gather fruits and wild berries to eat.

At this point, life was okay. We had access to shelter, food, and water. However, despite having the necessary factors for survival, many of us began to suffer emotionally. Several children began to break down and wonder about where our parents and families were located. After a while, child-like behavior combined with emotional turmoil began to take hold of our camps and soon everything began to turn into chaos. In addition to the emotional instability of our camp, disease began to spread. Some children became infected with, and died from Cholera, a deadly disease that occurs and develops from the consumption of unsanitary food or water. The rest of us were responsible for burying the bodies of those who had died.

We ended up living at our camp in the Ethiopian villages for approximately seven months. Then, we were eventually relocated to a formal refugee camp. At this point, news about the atrocities that happened to us was reaching international human rights organizations. As a result, some of the refugee camps began to receive aid and supplies. Unfortunately, the camp we were living at was too far away and received no support.

The Return to Sudan

After we lived at that camp for about a year, civil war began to erupt in Ethiopia. Unlike the civil war in Sudan that resulted from the government in the north with Arab Group International jihad upon southern Sudan; the civil war in Ethiopia was the result of political instability. Rebels who opposed the government of Ethiopia arrived at the camp in which we were living. We were once again forced to flee, this time back toward the Gila River which we crossed many months prior.

The rebels opened fire upon us and we were forced once again to cross the Gila River, this time back into Sudan. Many children died again while trying to cross the river. The rebel soldiers opened fire on us, but compared to the first time we crossed the Gilo River into Ethiopia, this time was nowhere near as terrifying. Although the soldiers used AK-47's and machine guns, they had no helicopters in their arsenal, resulting in a significantly less terrifying experience.

Although we arrived back into our home nation of South Sudan, we remained refugees. At this point in time, the civil war was still occurring. Many of our home villages were either under northern government control, in which sharia law was enacted, or our villages were in the center of conflict and war.

Somewhere Safe

With Sudan remaining hostile toward us and Ethiopia rejecting us too, we were now on a journey to find a new safe haven. We began to trek south across Sudan towards Kenya. This journey ahead of us would take approximately seven months to complete.

By the time we arrived in Kenya, some of us were so skinny we were literary walking skeletons. When we arrived, I was now five years old. Although I was young, I possessed great life experiences from the hardships experienced by my tribe and myself.

After seven months of traveling, we arrived in Kenya. We settled at a refugee camp located in the northern regions of Kenya. When we arrived, we were finally safe from the injustices and violence we had suffered at home in Sudan and in Ethiopia. However, we still had hardships ahead of us, but we survived and thrived the best we could with what we had.

The local populations in the Kenyan villages were apprehensive towards us as a result of us moving into their lands and using their natural resources–such as food and water – which were already in short supply. Even with the hatred from the locals, we began to build our lives with the limited resources we had. We began to develop our education. When we first arrived in Kenya, we were taught how to read and write. However, we had no paper or writing utensils at our disposal, so we improvised. We would take sticks and begin to write in the soil.

Overtime, the news of the atrocities that had happened to my people reached the international community, and aid began to flow in to help us. One specific memory I have is receiving real paper and writing supplies from the United Nations Children's Fund. This gift of paper and pencils allowed the other boys and me the opportunity to advance our education. We continued to study with the supplies given to us until we were able to read and write in English.

While living in Kenya, I developed an interest in learning music in addition to learning English. I also began to learn how to sing and play the organ. In 1999, while living in Kenya, my grandmother, who had also survived the atrocities that occurred back home in Sudan, passed away. Before she passed away, I made a promise to her that I would complete my education. I remember her telling me "My son, in the ages to come, education will be the only father and mother to you; you have no one left and for this, you must struggle to complete your education."

Resettlement to the United States

Between 2000 and 2001, The United States granted the opportunity for 3,600 of the Lost Boys and Girls of Sudan, including myself, to be resettled into the United States. During the process of resettlement to the United States, 99 percent of everyone resettled were males. In Sudanese culture – especially amongst the Nilotic people– girls are valued highly compared to the boys. As a result, few tribes were willing to give up their young girls and women for a study abroad program.

Upon arriving in the United States, I began to experience many things I had never seen or heard of before. One of the first things I remember that was different in the Northern United States compared to Sudan was the winter season. In Sudan, the temperature usually lingers around one hundred degrees or greater. I remember how cold the first winter in the United States felt, especially in comparison to the hot days back home in Sudan.

Another memory that clearly comes to mind was the quality and quantity of food available in the United States. I remember trying all of the foods that I had never had before; pizza was my favorite.

In addition to the cold winters and abundances of new foods to try, many of the newly resettled Lost Boys began to learn how to live with great amounts of new technology. It was the first time that many of us had encountered technology that American children had been exposed to all their lives; stoves, electricity, modern running water and plumbing, and even cereal boxes were new to us.

After being safely established in America, the call within me became too loud to ignore. In preparation for responding to that call, I went to school to learn all I could about world affairs and conflict resolution. Prior to my arrival in the States, I had little knowledge of this country. The move to a different social climate was a great culture shock. One of his greatest challenges was transitioning from full autonomy to living as part of a family system under their rules and expectations. I could scarcely remember what it was like to rely on parents and to be a child. I had been functioning as an independent adult since the age of five.

Being thrust into a totally new environment, I was learning new things every day, ranging from how to use the bus system to learning a new language. While most high school students go home after school, I received tutoring, attended ESL classes, and worked full time at a gas station. I was thirsty for knowledge and eager to learn. Unlike many teenagers in the United States who took education for granted, I recognized school for what it was – a great privilege and a massive gift.

Eventually my hard work paid off; by the time I completed high school my English was fluent. This love for learning has remained with me! I've served as a human rights officer within the Diocese of Kansas City-St. Joseph (Missouri); I have worked as a manager at Price Chopper, an employment specialist at Catholic Charities of Northeast Kansas. I have worked as a teacher at the Youth Science Institute and as a legislative intern for the United States Senate in Washington, DC. My varied work has broadened my level of experience and has equipped me to communicate effectively with individuals of all socioeconomic and racial strata.

I now work for Bethany Christian Service. I've spent seven years working in the non-profit world, and somewhere along the line I've developed a heart for immigrants and refugees.

John Deng Langbany

There is also John Deng Langbany, who appeared on the Public Broadcasting Service (PBS): "My first childhood memory began when I was about five years old in my homeland of Sudan; the day when my parents' house was burned. It was the last day I saw them. I ran with thousands of other young children in a very hard journey across the desert all the way to Ethiopia. I was small so the other children carried me there. I have many memories of my time in Ethiopia. I survived through the worst sort of life."

"Every day people were dying. I was living with a group of children in Panyido, Ethiopia who had also lost their families. In Panyido, I couldn't do a lot of the things that the other children did because I was the youngest. For example, when they swam in the river I couldn't do it because the crocodiles would pick on me. I was scared all the time. I was good at climbing trees, but not at swimming. One day I decided to cross the river with a few of my friends who carried me across so we could get to a tree to catch some mongoose. Somebody came with a gun and shot at us in the tree. He was an Ethiopian who hated us. We all had to jump down. We fell into the river. When I jumped into the river, I went too deep and my stomach was bleeding and I couldn't breathe. I thought I wouldn't live anymore. It was painful. One of my friends was killed and one kid drowned in the water. They never found his body. I lived."

"In 1991, when the government of Ethiopia fell apart, the new government chased us out of Panyido. We were chased to the edge of a big river that ran very fast, called Gilo. They kept shooting at us, so either you jumped in the water and they knew that you would drown because the water was way too fast, or you would be shot. I didn't know how to swim so all day I watched people being killed. There was a lot of crying. The people crossing the river had to throw all their bags away but it didn't do any good because the shooting continued. I was crying as people near me were being shot. The river was full of people. You realized later they were all dead. I needed to get across the river. I was thinking all day what I could do about it. I was too little and I didn't have parents to help me cross the river, and I didn't know whether my brother had already made it across. I remembered how the elders had shown us how to protect ourselves, so I covered myself with a person who was dead. When the shooting cooled down, I asked the boy next to me if he would try to cross the river with me. He didn't know how to swim either. I threw myself in. I don't know how, but the river was moving so fast it brought me to the other side. That's how I crossed the river that killed so many people."

"I followed the other children who survived to a place called Pachala. It took three days walking by foot. We didn't have water or anything. Pachala was on the Sudan side of the border with Ethiopia. When we got there, we saw hunger like I'd never seen in my life. There was no UN, no nothing. If you found one kernel of corn you lived off that for a day or two; water and a little corn. It was a tough life. We lived like that for two months. Then the UNHCR came in and started bringing food. Just as things got a little better with food, the enemy from Ethiopia crossed the border and the fighting began again. We had to leave Pachala. Before I could leave, one of the ladies told me to wait while everyone left so they could see if I could be carried out in a Red Cross car for the injured and the smallest children, so I stayed behind. A month after the rest of the kids had left, I was playing in the little river with the other children and the enemy came. While I was jumping in the water, I heard a sound. It was a bullet, but I didn't know what it was. When I got out of the water, the kids I was playing with were gone. I couldn't run because the bullets were all around me. I stayed flat and waited until night-time. It was dark. I escaped from the river to the airstrip. There was also shooting at the airstrip. I stayed down. I tried to go to my house. I didn't know that the people who were living with me were all gone. When I got to my house, I accidentally kicked a can and the enemy heard me. They captured me. They took me to the place where they had a lot of people they'd captured. I stayed there for most of the night. Sometime before morning hours, I escaped under the fence."

"I walked all the way to Oboth. On my way, I found one of my friends dead on the road. I had lived with him. His name was Mabil. It took me a long time to get to Oboth. On the way, there was a lot of shelling on the road. I thank God I was not killed. The shells missed me. When I got to Oboth, I met with the Sudanese people. I walked for three days to get to a place called Okila. I found the Sudanese Red Cross lady that had told me not to leave Pachala. She was still alive. I was happy. From there, we went to a place called Buma. In Buma, I found the UN and they announced that they would take the little children. At night, we were trying to sleep but some people came and shot at us. Three of my friends were killed. One was my father's brother-in-law. He was sleeping in the same bed as my brother, but my brother Aleer Gideon did not get shot. I ran into a tent but I didn't know there was a cooking fire inside. I threw myself in the fire to escape the shooting. I was burned. In the morning, after we got shot at, we left Magose to go to Kapoeta. We didn't stop there. We were with Red Cross vehicles and we went all the way to Nairus. There was no food for a while. The UN had to come in and give us food."

"While we were in Nairus, the enemy captured Kapoeta again so the UN decided to bring us to Lokichiogio across the border into Kenya. When we came to Lokichiogio, we lived there but were still scared that something might happen again so the UN decided to bring us Kakuma, Kenya further in from the border. This was in 1992. In Kakuma, the native people treated us badly because they didn't know us. They were nomadic people called Turkana. They didn't know

Sudanese. In 1994, I went back to Sudan. In 1995, I went to Ifo in Kenya. I lived in a refugee camp there trying to find a way to get to America. Three years later, I flew out of Nairobi to America and started high school in Rochester, Minnesota. I didn't know if I would find a good way of living anymore before I came to America. When I graduated from high school, I started community college and now I'll be going to Winona State University."

"It took me a long time to realize that I have gained a lot from living with so many people in the refugee camps. Nobody can believe it that I can speak fourteen different languages. It was a part of learning while going through bad things. You can go through a lot but one day things can change. With my classmates, I don't compare myself to them. I didn't have a good life when I was a young kid, but today I've learned more and I have a good life. This is a summary of my experiences but there is more to explain for each example I've given. I'm so glad I'm still alive and this is my story."

Bol Aweng

Bol Aweng was also resettled in the United States where he becamea successful painter. Recently, he shared his story. Bol Aweng was forced from his home in Sudan when he was six-years-old. As a child, he faced violence at the hands of government soldiers, danger from wild animals, starvation, and disease. His was an odyssey that eventually came to the United States, where he now uses his experience and education to help others.

Aweng, also one of the Lost Boys of Sudan, recently spoke at the Holy Family Church in Stow, Ohion. He is now an Ohio-based artist who has used his personal success to give back to those less fortunate in his native country.

"I spent twenty years not knowing if my family was alive or not," said Aweng, who travelled on foot 1,500 miles to Ethiopia and then to Kenya, all in all spending fourteen years in refugee camps. He came to the United States in 2001, eventually becoming a U.S. citizen and gaining a college education.

As a six-year-old, Aweng's job in his village was to take care of one hundredcows, providing water and food, among other chores. Caring for these cows may have saved his life when the soldiers descended upon his village in 1987.

As soon as they heard the gunshots, violence and havoc erupted. Aweng fled with a group of survivors. Their journey was dangerous from the start. "Many who could not make it were left behind," Aweng said. "And everyone who was left behind was left behind forever."

Lion attacks were on their minds, so the villagers would climb trees or make a lot of noise as they travelled. Aweng explained that although they were safe from lions, other animals could still climb trees. It was at this point that he realized, "Only God would provide a safe place."

Starvation and disease also followed the group. They had to grab whatever was available, which usually included leaves, roots and wild fruit. Some of these things, however, were poisonous, which Aweng discovered the hard way. He accidentally ate something that made him so sick that he was unconscious for almost twenty four hours.

He shared an especially touching story about an older child who looked out for him when he was six. The nine-year-old kept telling him there was candy in the next village, which would give Aweng enough motivation to keep going. The older boy looked after him, but eventually he contracted the measles and died during the group's pilgrimage. "Me and some other boys took him to the crypt," said Aweng, tearing up over the memory. "That was painful."

After four years at a refugee camp in Ethiopia, because the country was facing its own civil war, Aweng and his companions were forced back into Sudan. He recalled a poignant moment as they were forced to cross the Gilo River to go to the other side.

Those who could not swim drowned, "just like that." Some were dragged away by the current, and then eaten by crocodiles. "Crossing the Gilo was the largest moment of my life," said Aweng, who admitted he wasn't a good swimmer so his choices were grim. He had to either face being shot or jump into the river.

The walk back to Sudan was as dangerous as the journey away from it. One night the group dropped down into a dry riverbed to sleep, only to be ambushed by government soldiers. Many of the villagers were shot during the night. Aweng awoke with blood covering him, but it wasn't his. The blood belonged to a friend sleeping nearby, who never woke up.

This time, the group fled to Kenya. The road was rocky and painful, especially for those without shoes.

"When our number was counted again, we ended up with sixteen thousand," he said, "nineteen thousandwere missing, from the shooting, because of crocodiles or lions, or due to hunger and disease."

Aweng remained in Kenya for ten years. For the first time in ages, his community was free to gather in a large group to celebrate events like Christmas and to hold marches. Before, if they congregated in groups that were too large, the government would target them.

"In 2001, I made it to the United States," he said. "I was so excited when I received the letter."

His trip to New York City was held up by something unexpected and he was detained in Sudan for four days. "That was Sept. 11, 2001," he said, adding that he couldn't help but feel that war was following him, even all the way to the United States.

Eventually, Aweng resettled in Nashville, Tennessee, at the age of 20. Adapting to life in the U.S. presented its own set of challenges, he said. He saw a computer for the first time and learned that he could perhaps use this technology to tell people around the world about the crisis in Sudan, in order to help his countrymen there.

Aweng decided to express himself and his journey using art. He began by painting the wild animals of his native country on rocks. He graduated from Ohio State University in 2009 with a degree in digital art and went on to illustrate a children's book entitled, *Maluak's Cows*, which tells the story of the Lost Boys of South Sudan. He now lives in Columbus, Ohio.

When he became a U.S. citizen, Aweng said he finally felt like he had an identity and could stop looking behind his back for looming danger.

Aweng returned to Sudan in 2007, visiting his village of Piol. There he found his parents and reconnected with family members. But other parts of the trip weren't so positive. There were no buildings due to the bombing, only huts, there were no schools and very little food. "When I looked at what used to be my village, it was just a blank background," he said. There was nothing left. "Everything was destroyed."

While back in Sudan, he also noticed that the local healthcare workers only had a second-grade education. This was the person in charge of reading prescription drug labels and dispensing medicine to the community.

Said Aweng: "One out of five children in South Sudan do not live to age five." He became part of a group dedicated to founding the Buckeye Health Clinic in Sudan, which focuses on maternal and child health. In June, 2012, the Maternal and Child Health Care building was completed.

As an aside, villagers were given Ohio State Buckeye T-shirts, and the villagers told Aweng, "If you bring us a medical clinic, then we could call that medical clinic a Buckeye." The villagers were skeptical at first, because others had promised similar improvements, but Aweng's team made good on their word.

Villagers soon saw medical advancements, such as the installation of a "cold chain" in order to keep vaccines and other medications at safe temperatures, and proper care for mothers and babies.

South Sudan is still in crisis, however. Aweng said that even though the country separated from North Sudan in 2011, internal strife developed within South Sudan's government, leading to armed conflict in 2013, and displacing five hundred thousand civilians.

His message to the audience: "Go out and help" (Akronist.com). Aweng has been able to do something meaningful with his life because he was helped by the UNHCR. He knows that it is part of his mission in life to help others, so he is calling on everyone to help people around the world who are in need.

Salva Dut

Salva Dut, the director for the East African operations of Water for South Sudan, a humanitarian aid organization, was also one of the Lost Boys. This is his story which was published on the Water for South Sudan's website.

In 1985, Salva, then just eleven years old, was one of the seventeen thousand Lost Boys of Sudan who fled that country's southern region during Sudan's two-decade civil war. During their flight, a significant number of the Lost Boys perished from hunger, thirst, disease as well as attacks by wild animals and military attacks. Among the lucky survivors, Salva escaped to the relative safety of Ethiopia and later to Kenya. As a teenager in 1990, Salva led about one thousand five hundred of the Lost Boys from Ethiopia across hundreds of desert miles southwest through Sudan to the United Nations-controlled Kakuma refugee camp near the Kenyan city of Lodawar. He lived in the barbed-wire-enclosed camp along with ninety two thousand other refugees for nearly six years. In 1996, under the auspices of the U.S. State Department and the United Nations, about three thousand eight hundred of the Lost Boys, including Salva, came to the United States, while others went to Australia and Canada. Arriving in the US in 1996, Salva spoke little English and lacked formal education.

Salva's family members who survived the war and remained in Southern Sudan thought he was dead. But, in the US, Salva was determined to somehow reconnect with them. Eventually Salva Dut founded and served as Executive Director for East Africa Operations of Water for South Sudan, Inc. In January 2002, Salva learned from a fellow refugee that his father, Mawien Dut, was seriously ill in a UN clinic, which he'd reached after walking 300 miles. Sensing that this could be the last opportunity to reunite with his father, Salva returned to Sudan. The two had not seen each other in over sixteen years. There he discovered that his father was suffering from waterborne parasites and disease.

There was no clean water in his father's village. Once reunited with Salva and healthy again, the elder Dut abandoned his life-long home and moved about a hundred miles away to where he could find clean water.

Salva's trip reconnected him to the harsh truth of everyday life for the people of South Sudan who lack access to safe, fresh water. Grateful to the American people who had helped him change his own life, he returned to the US determined to make a difference for the people of his birthplace. He and a small group of friends founded Water for South Sudan Inc. in 2003, to raise funds and drill water wells. This has become Salva's life mission.

Salva became an American citizen and studied International Business in Rochester, New York, while working as president and drilling manager of Water for South Sudan Inc. He moved back to South Sudan following his nation's independence in July, 2011 and now oversees Water for South Sudan's operations in Africa. Salva's heroic personal story and authentic humble character inspires audiences to support the organization's humanitarian mission of service to the people of South Sudan.

Shimma

Shimma is another Lost Boy. His tribal home is in Sudan. He is believed to be twenty one and has lived as a refugee in the USA since August 2001.

I met Shimma while shopping at Walmart in central Phoenix. I had been fascinated by the reports of the Lost Boys that I had heard on television and had read in the newspaper. I knew that some of the Lost Boys were being relocated to Phoenix and hoped to meet some of them as I travelled there. I had seen a few at bus stops and around the city. These young men have a very distinctive appearance and are not your typical African-American. They are tall and thin with high cheekbones and a dark black skin tone.

While shopping at Walmart, I rounded a corner and there he stood, tall, dark and smiling. I was excited about finally meeting one of the Lost Boys and began to ramble, introducing myself and inquired about his status as one of the Lost Boys. He introduced himself and confirmed that he was indeed one of the Lost Boys I had been reading and hearing about. I requested an interview and he offered his name and telephone number. After weeks of reaching him by phone he agreed to meet me at a local restaurant. On the day of our interview he arrived more than an hour late, which I dismissed as a cultural difference. However, Shimma is a very busy man. He works at Walmart and attends ESL classes two days a week at Phoenix Community College.

Shimma was given the birth date of January 1, 1982 because there is no birth certificate or official date of birth for a tribal child in Sudan. His middle name is Gatkuoth, the name of his father and his last name is Puot the name of his grandfather. He speaks five languages beginning with his tribal village language of Nuer, his next language is Anoak a Sudanese language and then Amaric, which is Ethiopian. He also speaks Arabic and English. His family was large; his father had six wives and twenty one children. Shimma was born to his third wife along with four sisters and three brothers.

If Shimma had been able to remain in Sudan, his life would have been very different from the American culture that he lives in today. He would have joined with the groups of patriarchal elders who lead the clans. He speaks with affection of his native people's kindness and generosity. He tells of their willingness to kill and share a goat with travelers. Sub-clans such as the Bantu, Lounuer, Gajioke and more, surround his tribal village of Nuer. His family and neighbors were all interrelated through geographic identification.

When young men reach the age of maturity, they are brought into this rite by the tribal custom of pulling the lower incisor teeth and at about the age of twenty one, or manhood, scars are placed on the forehead signifying his manhood. Boys were sent to the fields to herd cattle and the women and girls remained in the village. This is how many escaped the massacres in the villages. Marriage required a long courtship. Years of simple conversation culminated in asking permission of tribal elders for permission to marry. Wedding tradition demanded that cattle be given to the men in the wives' family in exchange for the wife. Fathers, uncles and brothers all received cattle in exchange for the bride.

Shimma's Christian village was burned and destroyed by the Islamic regime army. His father was killed and Shimma barely escaped after being shot in the leg. He escaped with his uncle who helped carry him across the dangerous deserts. Many dangers awaited them in the deserts of Sudan. Tigers, lions and poisonous snakes took the lives of many of the boys on the journey. Shimma and his uncle survived by eating the root of the Deony tree. He does not know how long they walked he just knows that it was a long, long journey to Ethiopia.

When they arrived in Ethiopia they were given an axe with which to build a shelter and survived on one meal a day of lentils and wheat. He still rarely eats more than once a day even in a land of abundance. During his stay in the Ethiopian camp by some strange twist of bad luck he was hit by lightning and paralyzed on his left side for months. He has since recovered completely. When the regime changed in Ethiopia they were sent out of the camp at gunpoint, some were shot, others were forced into the river and drowned. Many were attacked and killed by crocodiles and hippos. Shimma's uncle constructed a grass mat that floated down and across the river. He returned seven times saving many lives through his courage and heroism. He rescued many from death.

After being forced back into Sudan, Shimma attempted to locate his mother and his siblings. Nobody knew of their whereabouts. He began to walk again. This time his arduous journey led him to Kenya and a huge refugee camp in

Kakuma. Of seventeen thousand boys, only ten thousand survived to make the journey to Kenya. The rest died of starvation, thirst, attacks by wild animals, bombings, and despair. The war continued and hope of repatriation faded. Shimma remained in limbo, stuck between countries and homes, life and death, until 2001. The refugee process is long and many along the way assisted him.

Today Shimma lives with friends, other Lost Boys, in an apartment. He has learned to ride the bus, drive a car, and hold down a job. As with other transnational villagers, he hopes to return home someday and continues to send money to his uncle who is attending university in Ethiopia. He sends $300 a month out of his meager Walmart earnings. He plans to achieve the highest degree possible, a PhD, and return to Sudan to help his people. He likes burgers and burritos. He hates the noise of the city and has no interest in drinking or drugs.

He attends Phoenix College, taking ESL classes two days a week. He is respectful and kind. His faith is strong. He believes that God saved him and, God willing, he will one day return home. I believe he will make it.

Some of these "Lost Boys of Sudan" have made up a large portion of the Church of Sudan. Even though some of them were earlier devoted to the native religions, there are a good number who are Christians. Whenever their stories are told, lives are changed. These people were chosen by God to be evangelists through their lives. The work of international organizations in the lives of the people of South Sudan also testifies to the Lord's goodness in their lives.

The Sudanese

The people of Sudan have conducted themselves properly in the face of the persecutions they have endured. One might wonder from whence their courage came, had not the stories in the Bible been provided for us. These scriptures instruct us in the ways of the Lord and his Spirit.

It is apparent, as the preceding chapters have manifested, that the people of Sudan are a people who love the Lord wholeheartedly and have always reached out to support the desire of the Lord. It is, therefore, no surprise to find that about ten million people of Cush are submitting themselves to God. There has recently been tremendous church-growth in Southern Sudan. Some pastors have reported adding over eight thousand people to their churches in just three years. Numerous pastors have multiple congregations to care for.

The resilient Christians of Sudan have stood steadfast against the onslaught of Islamic Jihad. They have served as a bulwark, restraining the southward expansion of Islam in Africa. Straddling the Nile, these Christian tribes have frustrated the ambitions of Islamic Jihadists in Khartoum.

The bishops of the Episcopal Church, and the Roman Catholic Church, and the Christian chiefs refused to submit, and instead, in an impressive show or display of bravado, declared on the sixteenth of May, 1983, that they would not abandon God as God had revealed himself to them in Jesus Christ. Over the next twenty two long years of intense misery and aggravated pain, every house, school, clinic, church and public building was burned to the ground in an area the size of Texas. The barbarousness was so terrible that six million people were displaced, four million of which fled to other countries, and two and a half million were killed.

As of 1983, only five percent of the population was Christian. The irony of the injustice that took place is quite beyond the fathoming of sociological experts and can only be explained by the exploration of Biblical history and prophecies. Today, there are about five million Episcopalians, and a whooping three million Roman

Catholics representing 95 percent of the people. Not only has the church in Sudan survived the furious fires of persecution, but they have thrived, even winning some of their enemies to Christ.

In July 2011, South Sudan became the 192nd new sovereign republic of the world with 95 percent of its Christians rejuvenating their faith. Throughout the process of Arabization that has been taking place in Sudan, even more people seem to be embracing Christianity. Statistics support this observation. The number of Christians in Sudan has increased from 1.6 million in 1980 to 11 million in 2010.

Every chapter, each phase, each facet of the Sudan massacre carries stories of some of the four million martyrs and the conditions of their deaths. These disasters are like the phoenix, which is usually reborn from the ashes of its previous deaths, becoming stronger life after life. As hard as these tragedies and disasters are to witness, they have been transformed over and over again to become the seeds of unshakable faith and joy. This is truly a mystery of faith. The events of the martyrdoms became the foundation upon which to reflect how the continued impact their lives have in feeding, not only the church in the Sudan, but throughout the world.

APPENDIX

There are several organizations dedicated to restoring Sudan and her people.

Save Darfur

One helpful organization is the Save Darfur Movement (savedarfur.org). Although people may hold reservations about this organization, they are at least doing *something* to help the people of Sudan. They are bringing hope and love to a people displaced by war and ravaged by famine, disease, and hunger.

The Save Darfur Coalition was founded at the Darfur Emergency Summit, held in New York City on July 14, 2004. It has since grown into an alliance of more than one hundred and eighty religious, political and human rights organizations committed to ending the alleged genocide in Darfur. The Save Darfur Coalition is headquartered in Washington, D.C., with a staff of thirty professional organizers, policy advisors, and communications specialists.

The coalition's members have agreed to the following unity statement:

"We stand together and unite our voices to raise public awareness and mobilize a massive response to the atrocities in Sudan's western region of Darfur. Responding to a rebellion in 2003, the regime of Sudanese President Omar al-Bashir and its allied militia, known as the Janjaweed, launched a campaign of destruction against the civilian population of ethnic groups identified with the rebels. They wiped out entire villages, destroyed food and water supplies, stole livestock and systematically murdered, tortured and raped civilians. The Sudanese government's genocidal, scorched earth campaign has claimed hundreds of thousands of lives through direct violence, disease and starvation, and continues to destabilize the region. Millions have fled their homes and live in dangerous camps in Darfur, and hundreds of thousands are refugees in neighboring Chad. Violence continues today. Ultimately, the fate of the Darfurian people depends on establishing a lasting and just peace in all of Sudan and in the region.

We are committed to:
Ending the violence against civilians;
Facilitating adequate and unhindered humanitarian aid;
Establishing conditions for the safe and voluntary return of displaced people to their homes;
Promoting the long-term sustainable development of Darfur; and
Holding the perpetrators accountable.

We call on the United States, other governments, the United Nations and regional organizations to focus their efforts on ending this crisis."

Human Rights Watch

The Human Rights Watch (hrw.org) is a watchdog organization that has greatly helped the people of Sudan. The staff consists of human rights professionals including: country experts, lawyers, journalists, and academics of diverse backgrounds and nationalities. Established in 1978, Human Rights Watch is known for its accurate fact-finding, impartial reporting, effective use of media, and its targeted advocacy, often in partnership with local human rights groups. The organization meets with governments, the United Nations, regional groups like the African Union and the European Union, financial institutions, and corporations to press for changes in policy and practice that promote human rights and justice around the world. Their work is guided by respect for the dignity of each human being.

Help Arises – Human Rights Watch

Whenever there is any issue in the Sudan, these people never fail to take the matter up personally, carrying out careful investigations. This is the type of external attention that influenced and prompted the International Crimes Court to sit on the case of Sudan. A panel of three judges issued an arrest warrant for the president of Sudan, Omar al-Bashir on seven counts of war and war crimes, but he retaliated by expelling the aid organizations from his country, accusing them of feeding the world with false information about Sudan.

International Rescue Committee

Another organization committed to providing aid to Sudan is the International Rescue Committee, IRC (www.rescue.org). Since December, 2013, after a political rivalry between South Sudan's president and a former vice president, erupted into violence, thousands of people have been killed and some 2 million have been forced to flee their homes. The IRC is providing urgently needed medical care, water and sanitation services, protection for vulnerable women and girls, and other assistance.

The story of the Sudanese people is moving organizations all over the world to sympathy. People are rising up to give them hope in these desperate times. The Sudanese are not alone in their struggle. The world is standing with them.

PART

II:

THE CAUSES OF WAR

CHAPTER 12:

THE LARGEST COUNTRY DIVIDED

History of Arabization: The Ancient World

Arabization is not a new concept to Sudan, but rather an issue that has been affecting the region for centuries. Before Arabization penetrated Africa, the established culture stretched north along the Nile River and into Egypt where it held political power for a century (Kendall). Before the year 400 A.D., the area where Northern Sudan now exists was home to Nubia, an ancient and Middle Ages kingdom that ran along the Nile River. The kingdom of Nubia expanded from what is now central and southern Egypt into current-day northern Sudan. The Nubia kingdom was comprised of a number of smaller kingdoms along the Nile River. These included Kerma, Kush, Dotawa, Makuria, Nobadia, and Alodia.

During the fourth century, the kingdom of Aksum invaded Nubia, causing its collapse. Aksum reigned for almost a thousand years beginning on the eastern edge of the Nile River and expanding through modern day northern Ethiopia to the Red Sea and on into the Arabian Peninsula to an eastern political border near modern day Khamis Mushait in Saudi Arabia.

Following the collapse of Meroe and the Nubia kingdom, three new kingdoms arose out the fallen larger nation. They consisted of Nobadia in the north, located south of Egypt at modern day Faras in southern Egypt; Makuria, which was located on the border between southern Egypt and Northern Sudan, and Alodia, located where Sudan stands today (Spaulding, 1995).

During the fourth through eighth centuries, the three new kingdoms were exposed to Christianity and the life-saving knowledge of Christ's death on the cross. The news of Christ was brought to the new kingdoms through priests and missionaries from the north. Between the years 350 A.D. and 800 A.D., the three kingdoms were officially declared Christian, asserting allegiance to the Greek Church and the Coptic Orthodox Church (one of the largest Christian churches operating in Egypt and the Middle East).

In the seventh century, Arabic Muslims invaded from the east. The attacks began in 641 A.D. and lasted through Egypt's conquest in 651 A.D. (Spaulding, 1995). This invasion signified the first instance of Arabization on the African cotenant. During the Muslim conquests, the kingdom of Makuria effectively resisted the Muslim conquest during the first battle of Dongola in 642 A.D. and the second battle, fought a decade later in 652 A.D.

The result created the Baqt treaty, which resulted in peace between the militaries of the newly Arabized Egyptians to the north and the Makuria kingdom. The peace between them lasted until the thirteenth century. Despite this, there were cultural invasions that impacted the nations along the Nile. Within the Baqt treaty, the new Arabs to the region were allowed to live among and intermingle with the existing culture. This involved allowing the sale and trade of slaves to the new Arabic residents (Spaulding, 1995). This was the first instance in which Africans were slaves to Arabic cultures, and eventually had dramatic impact on the lives of the citizens of South Sudan.

South of Makuria lay the kingdom of Alodia, the most southern of the three Nubia kingdoms, located in modern day Sudan. At the southern tip of the Nubia kingdoms, Alodia was the last one to receive the message of Christ (Shinnie, 1996. P. 133), brought there during the seventh century by missionaries from the Roman Empire. Alodia remained a Christian kingdom for almost one thousand years.

After the Arabic invasions along the Nile River into the Nubia kingdoms during the seventh century, the Church of Nubia lost its contacts and connections with the other churches located throughout the Middle East and Europe.

Between the seventh and sixteenth centuries, the Nubia kingdoms thrived but were significantly influenced with by the Arabic world. During this time, Arabic officials, Arabic culture, and Islam began to infiltrate the political and cultural aspects of the kingdom; new laws and policies negatively impacted the lives of non-Arabs and non-Muslims. Those who opposed the Arabic culture were forced to pay higher taxes than those of Arabic decent. Political leaders who were not of Arabic decent were forced from their posts. During the late tenth and early eleventh centuries, Christians and others who did not adapt to the Arabic culture were violently persecuted (BBC, no. 1).

Soon Arabization began to impact other cultural aspects, including the architecture, now becoming traditionally Arabic. Houses built for Arabic officials now featured red brick and large domes, similar to those in Iraq (Salih).

By the fifteenth century, the remaining kingdoms of the Nubia Empire eventually fell, after which an increasing number of Arabians continued to arrive in the region, which was then divided among these new arrivals. This would continue until the beginning of the nineteenth century.

History of Arabization: The Ottoman Empire

The last of the Nubia kingdoms collapsed at the beginning of the sixteenth century. Between then and eighteenth centuries, the Ottoman Empire conquered much of northern Africa. As previously experienced, the invaders brought their culture to pass onward to the local communities.

By the beginning of the nineteenth century, Mohammed Ali – a high ranking officer in the Ottoman Empire – rose to power in Egypt and sent his military into the Southern Sudan to territory that belonged to the Dinka Tribe (BBC, no.2). There, the soldiers searched for new slaves to ship back to Egypt. This invasion from the Ottoman Empire would be told for generations amongst my tribe. It was referred to as "the time when the earth became spoiled."

British Control

During the remainder of the nineteenth century, conflict continued in Sudan, waged between the African tribes in Southern Sudan and the Arabic invaders from Egypt and Northern Sudan. Eventually, the Africans subdued the Arabic forces. However, by the end of the nineteenth century, British forces began to grow increasingly interested in the occupation of Sudan. As a result, they launched campaigns to gain control of the area (Sudan: History, 2007). This resulted in many hostilities toward the British. My tribe and the other natives of South Sudan were faced with the hardships of colonization. The Arabs and Egyptians who lived in Northern Sudan also resented the occupation, since they also wanted to control the country.

Both the African-controlled Southern Sudan and the Arabic-controlled Northern Sudan resented the British control. Before long the British forces began to separate the nation into two different sections. As a result, the British administration began to split the management of the two regions.

This led to increased attempts at Arabization during the second half of the twentieth century. In 1952, conflict and revolutions increased in Egypt, resulting in the British Government relinquishing colonial control of Sudan and returning authority to the citizens. The northern Arabic regions gained control of the country, because they had greater wealth than the African-controlled Southern Sudan.

By 1956 the African South began to fear dominance by the Arabic North, which possessed a significantly greater amount of wealth and resources than southern Sudan. The South feared North would force their Arabic culture upon the African South.

Soon there was talk of a federal system between the north and the south, which led to conflict within the Equatorial region, an area located at the southernmost borders of Sudan. The conflicts began as guerrilla efforts by the South Sudan military to resist Arabization and to obtain independence (Global Security, 2012). These efforts would eventually expand into a civil war, which would last for seventeen years and claim a vast number of lives.

Arabization and the First Civil War Causes of War: Slavery

Slavery has existed in Sudan for over a thousand years. More than ninety-five percent of the enslaved have been of African descent. However, no Sudanese government has ever allowed those of Arabic decent to become enslaved. During the second Sudanese Civil War, when the military forces from Northern Sudan invaded my village and the villages of my tribe, many women and children were taken into slavery. The women were raped and the children were forced into tedious, manual labor. Now, however, many organizations in the international community have become aware of modern day slavery and are paying greater attention. Such organizations include Christian Solidarity Worldwide, Christian Freedom International, and Persecution. Other, non-faith based organizations paying attention to this modern day crisis are the United Nations and the Human Rights Watch. Despite this expanded knowledge, slavery continues.

Slavery before the Second Civil War

Slavery in Sudan dates back to the ancient world. The first instance occurred as the result of military conflicts between African kingdoms, such as the Nubians and the ancient Egyptian Empire. The winning side took prisoners of war, who they forced into slavery (Labb, 2004).

During the Arabic invasions into Africa in the middle of the seventh century, the "Baqt Treaty" was signed to establish peace between the Christian Nubian kingdoms and the invading Arabic kingdoms. Under the treaty the sale and trade of slaves was permitted (Spaulding, 1995) in order to maintain peace between the Christian Makuria Kingdom and the invading Muslims; Makuria was now forced to deliver an annual payment of three hundred and sixty slaves to the invading Muslims and forty slaves directly to the governor of Egypt. This was agreed upon to maintain peace and halt future invasions (Vantini, 1981). Soon afterward, the Muslim and Arabic invaders began to acquire black Sudanese slaves, after which slaves became a significant commodity in the Middle East. Those acquired from the Makuria kingdom were relocated and forced to either work in mining jobs in what is now Southern Iraq or in labor in various salt mines in the Sahara (Lewis 1996).

After the Nubia kingdoms fell during the sixteenth century, slavery became a method for newly arising political powers to fill the ranks of their militaries (Freedom House). At the beginning of the nineteenth century, more than 5,000 slaves from the Sudan and the Middle East were sold each year at the market of Shendi (Eibner, 1999). By mid-nineteenth century, Mohammed Ali sent his forces from Egypt, which at that time was under control by the Ottoman Empire, into Southern Sudan to find slaves (BBC, no.2). During this invasion, slave traders in South Sudan would establish fortified camps in thorny brush called zaribas. From these places, slave traders and the forces from the Ottoman Empire abducted approximately 20,000 slaves to be shipped off to Egypt and other regions of the Middle East (Eibner, 1999).

When the British government colonized Sudan, they worked to put an end to the owning and sale of slaves and had strong connections with nineteenth-century, anti-slavery movements, including the Anti-Slavery Society (Eibner, 1999). Slavery was officially abolished in Sudan in 1898 (Sudan Update). Yet some instances were still reported until the 1920's. The Baqqara, a group of nomadic Arabic cattle herders in Northern Sudan, still abducted citizens from South Sudan and sold them in markets in the Middle East where the British Government was unable to track them (Henderson, 1965). Sudan remained free of slavery for almost an entire century.

During the first Sudanese civil war, there were only minimal reports of slavery. This was in the late 1950's. However, beginning in the middle of the 1980's, slavery began to occur once again and became a significant issue related to the second Sudanese civil war.

Slavery during the Second Civil War

During the second civil war, horrible atrocities occurred that impacted my life and the lives of my people. Although I was able to escape with a group of other boys that were located at the cattle camps of the City of Dong, many villagers were forced into slavery.

The conflict and raids upon our homes and villages began in 1983, the result of a surge in Islamic ideology in the Sudanese capital city of Khartoum. When Islamic political parties acquired greater control in Khartoum, they began to implement Sharia law upon the entire country, including the Christian population in the South. In response, the Sudan's Peoples' Liberation Movement/Army resisted the policies being forced upon them. As a result, the government took enhanced military action.

The government began to recruit Baqqara tribal militias, also called the Murahhilin, to wage war against anyone from the Dinka population located in the Bahr al-Ghazal region (Eibner, 1999). These slave raids were part of the government's effort against the Sudan's Peoples' Liberation Army. As the government supplied more fully automatic weapons to the Murahhilin, the slave raids became more bloody and violent. The government, in accordance to the Islamic doctrine of jihad, allowed these invaders to take any booty they collected from the raids. This included goats, cattle, grain, women, and children (Eibner, 1999, Frontline Fellowship).

This caused other African tribes and sub-tribes to join the Sudan's Peoples' Liberation Army to fight. When members of the Nuba tribes joined the ranks of the Sudan's

People's Liberation Army, the opposition responded by increasing their efforts and assaults on Sudanese villages. Now, even innocent civilians were labeled as infidels.

It still isn't known how many people were forced into slavery. The northern Sudanese government estimated that approximately five thousand people were abducted. However, many non-governmental organizations such as Anti-Slavery International have estimated the number to be more than a hundred thousand (PBS, 2003). This is in addition to an estimated two-million individuals who died during the second civil war and the four million others (including myself) who suffered displacement (Burr, 1998).

The slave raids that began in 1983 continued until 2002. One of the most violent raids occurred in the spring of 1998 when the Popular Defense Force, supported by the regular army, swept through Aweil West County, and penetrated deep inside Aweil West, Twic, and Abyei counties. Over three hundred thousand persons were displaced; the total number killed and enslaved is still not known. Slaves captured in this offensive later testified that thousands of women were placed in a pen, stripped of their clothing and videotaped by "Abd ar-Rahman Qidr, the government's commissioner in El Diein" (Eibner, 1999).

Approximately sixty percent of all of the women and children abducted during the course of the civil war were taken by tribal militias called the Murahaleen. Individuals who were abducted by the Murahaleen were taken primarily to the western regions of Kordofan and the southern regions of Darfur. Those from my tribe who were not abducted by the Murahaleen were, however, abducted by military forces including the Sudanese National Army and the Popular Defense Force (Anti-slavery).

The primary victims of slavery in Sudan were members of the Dinka tribe, the Joor, and those living in the Bahr el-

Ghazal region in Southern Sudan (Anti-slavery). Similar to what happened in the City of Dong, the Janjaweed attacked us. Darfur, located in western Sudan, also suffered attacks, and thousands of individuals are abducted and forced into slavery.

The most common abductees were children and women, ranging in age from toddler to forty. Generally, the children were beaten and forced into jobs that require extensive physical labor. Or they were forced to train as soldiers in the northern Sudanese military (PBS, 2003). The working conditions certainly violated labor laws advocated by the United Nations and modern society (Antislavery.org, 2001). The women, in addition to being beaten, were most often sexually abused, raped, and forced into marriages and hard labor ("Sudan's Slaves, adding...", 2008).

The invading forces typically killed men and older boys, because the Arab raiders knew it would take too much effort to force them into slavery and even more difficult to brainwash them into accepting a new ideology. Village elders who survived the raids were robbed and their homes were burned down (Frontline Fellowship).

The average slave in Sudan was sold for fifty dollars (Freedom Watch). Other reports indicate that in some situations a young male child would be offered as a gift to bribe a government official (PBS, 2003). In 1998, the United States State Department overheard radio communications in Sudan between Osama Bin Laden and other members of al Qaeda in which Osama Bin Laden was bartering one gun per slave to work on his marijuana farms in Sudan (PBS, 2003).

Some of the people abducted during the second civil war were forced into debt bondage or bonded labor, the most common form of slavery in the twenty-first century. It involves a person being forced into strenuous labor as a means to repay a loan. Typically, an individual is "tricked or trapped into working for very little or no pay, often for seven days a week. The value of the work is invariably greater than the original sum of money borrowed" (Anti-slavery, No. 2).

Even those who survived being abducted and taken into slavery are still suffering great hardships. Many who were separated from their families were shipped to areas where no one speaks their language. When the slaves either escaped or became free, they still had to overcome the hardships of having poor communication amongst different ethnic and cultural groups when trying to make their way back to their home village (Anti-slavery).

Responses to Slavery

Both during and after the second civil war, the attackers either ignored the international community's request to take action against the abductors or at times flat out denied that slavery was occurring. Beginning in 1996, caving to pressures of international organizations, the government responded by developing committees to investigate the accounts of slavery. However, the investigators claimed that the raids were not the responsibility of the governmental forces but rather the result of intertribal disputes and further maintained that people were taken as hostages, not as slaves (Sudan Update). Some families in my tribe, who have had their relatives kidnapped during the war, have attempted to navigate the Sudanese court system to have them returned. However, the court systems are as little help as the government is and acknowledge slaves as bonus perks to the soldiers that fought for the northern government.

Between December of 1998 and February of 1999, the Sudanese government and the Popular Defense Force agreed to a cease-fire. However, during this time period, a United Nations Children's Relief rapid response team assessed a reported incident of raiding. Their report found over two thousand people that had been taken into slavery and just less than two hundred killed during this attack (Lokichoggio, 1999).

Later in 1999 the Sudanese government told the United Nations that it was going to enact stronger enforcements and take additional action toward prosecuting any individual who was involved in the capture, sale, or trading of slaves. However, no one was ever brought to trial, and no charges were ever filed (Human Rights Watch, 2002).

In 2000, representatives, including a lawyer and an administrative director, from the international human rights organization Anti-Slavery International visited Khartoum to speak with Sudanese government officials about the subject of slavery in relation to the conflicts occurring in South Sudan since the 1980's. When they visited the Sudanese Ministry for External Relations, the deputy minister of the department and other officials "had been surprised when they first heard the allegations that slavery was occurring in Sudan" and then stated they did not believe such allegations.

Again, in 2001, the Sudanese government told the United Nations they were going to be more aggressive against those responsible for abductions, abuse, or forced labor. However, similar to what happened in 1999, the government never brought anyone to trial, and the human rights' violations continued (Human Rights Watch, 2002).

In 2002, the United States set up an international committee to help study the reported human rights violations and work with the Sudanese government on enforcing effective and practical policies and procedures to help bring those guilty to justice. However, when a group of seventeen citizens was massacred by government controlled helicopter gunship, the United States withdrew its efforts to help the Sudanese government bring anyone to justice (Human Rights Watch, 2002).

Other investigations of the slave trade in Sudan found that not only did the Government of Sudan turn a blind eye to the problem during the civil war, but in many instances it allowed slavery to occur. In fact, in 1995, evidence showed that the Government of Sudan had been taking four different steps to promote slavery among my people. First, the government had been equipping militias located in southern Darfur and southern Kordofan with fully automatic weaponry. The militias formed out of these regions would become the Popular Defense Force. Second, the Government of Sudan told the recruits that Sudanese citizens located in territories controlled by the Sudanese Peoples Liberation Army were associated with them and were enemies of Islam and granted permission to the Popular Defense Force to torture, kill, and enslave them. Thirdly, the government gave Popular Defense Force orders to attack specific villages and locations. This was what occurred during attacks at the City of Dong and the Cattle Camp where I was living. Fourthly, the Government of Sudan "[p]promised the raiders the right to keep whatever booty they could take, including human beings as slaves, in lieu of payment, in accordance with its doctrine of jihad" (Frontline Fellowship).

Because the systems established by the government offer little support in rescuing family members and seeing that they were able to return home, many Sudanese people have taken efforts into their own hands. Some villages in my tribe have spent hard-earned income to buy back slaves. A common occurrence is trading access to fresh water in exchange for the slaves. Although this has worked for some, it is more common for families to run into problems tracing down the slave masters. Even so, there is no guarantee they will free their slave.

CHAPTER 13:

THE PURCHASING
OF SLAVES

"States are made to serve people; governments are established to protect the citizens of a state against external enemies and internal wrongdoers. It is on these grounds that people surrender their right and power to self-defense to the government of the state in which they live. But when the whole machinery of the State, and the powers of the Government, is turned against a whole group of the society on the grounds of racial, tribal or religious prejudices, then the victims have the right to take back the powers they have surrendered, and to defend themselves. The basis of statehood, and of unity, can only be general acceptance by the participants if justice, equality, egalitarianism, freedom and social development are the practices of governments, and not only being beamed out as mere texts enshrined in constitutions. Surely, when more than twelve million people have become convinced that they are rejected in a country in which they live, and that there is no longer any basis for unity between them and other groups of people, then unity has already ceased to exist. You cannot kill thousands of people, and keep killing more, in the name of unity. There is no unity between the dead and those who killed them; and, worse still, there is no unity in slavery and domination."

Dr. John Garang, First President of the Republic of South Sudan

International Organizations Involvement: Purchasing Slaves

International non-governmental organizations have a long history of attempting to abolish slavery. During the Ottoman Empire's invasion into South Sudan during the nineteenth century, anti-slavery organizations in London advocated to end slavery (Fleuhr-Lobban, 1990). Today, many non-governmental organizations still work to this end.

In some instances, these groups have helped buy freedom for slaves at a typical cost of thirty-five to fifty dollars per person. However, as long as militia organizations exist and are encouraged by the northern government, slavery will continue to exist (Sudan Update).

Yet the international groups have much negotiation power in this process. An individual who owns slaves might be more willing to discuss their release with a larger organization than an individual family, community, sub-tribe, or tribe. The power of large organizations also allows for the freeing of a larger number of slaves.

In July of 2000, a United Kingdom group called Save the Children was able to locate and help free more than a thousand women and children (Anti-Slavery International, 2001). The group also freed 275 slaves in Northern Sudan.

Slave owners know large organizations also have significantly more resources than do individual families. Thus, many slave traders have been able to increase the price of a slave (Human Rights Watch, 2002). In other words, they now make a profit on selling people.

According to the Human Rights Watch, when third party organizations became involved in purchasing back slaves, fraud and corruption may have been involved. At times middlemen falsified information and kept the cash for themselves. In other instances, the Human Rights Watch has reported these middlemen pay local residents to pose as slaves. Then the international organization pays for their release, unaware they were being scammed. Of course, this takes from the money that could have paid for the release of actual slaves.

In July of 2000, Christian Solidarity International discovered a botched purchase. A hundred and thirty-three slaves who were freed went missing, never to be heard of again (Anti-Slavery International, 2001).

Some organizations have begun to buyback slaves using payment of British pounds instead of United States dollars. This helps to reduce the purchase of violent weapons. Because U. S. dollars have a greater liquidity than the British pound, the dollars are commonly used in black market trades for illegal fully automatic weaponry used by the militias and individuals in the Northern Sudanese Government conducting raids into South Sudan.

Many organizations trying to end slavery have run into opposition by the government. Christian Solidarity International, for instance, faced political opposition by the National Islamic Front that controlled the Sudanese government. Omar al-Bashir, president of Sudan during the majority of the second Sudanese civil war, protested to the United Nations. Omar al-Bashir lied to the United Nations in stating Christian Solidarity International was the organization responsible for the abduction and atrocities occurring in Southern Sudan (Yasin, 1999).

Organizations such as Anti-Slavery International have condemned efforts by other international organizations to re-purchase slaves. In addition to the principal that purchasing a slave increases price as a result of stimulated market demand, the re-purchase of slaves operates as a means for militias and others responsible for slavery to acquire wealth and additional resources that can be used in future raids and crimes of human rights. Although the re-purchase of slaves frees them, it offers no way to end a system that allows and promotes slavery (Anti-Slavery International, 2001).

Sudanese Involvement: The Dinka Committee

During the crises and hardship that my people suffered during the second Sudanese civil war, my tribe began to set up and develop a committee to work for the retrieval of abducted women and children. The Dinka Committee was started in the late 1980's by James Aguer. Its primary purpose is to track down missing tribal members, find those responsible for abducting them, and attempt to negotiate a price for their release.

The Dinka Committee estimated that about 14,000 members of my tribe were taken into slavery. Of those, an estimated 600 ended up in Darfur, and another 8,000 in Kordofan (Anti-Slavery International, 2001), far more than the northern government estimated. The Dinka Committee has been able to secure freedom for more than a thousand members. However, they have been met by strong opposition. When the group began to bring individuals home from the Darfur region, members of the local Rizeigat community were extremely helpful and cooperative; working hand-in-hand with the committee in identifying captured individuals for release. This worked well until Northern Sudanese Governmental forces found out what the committee was doing and discouraged such cooperation. In some instances, the government prevented the release of captive Dinka citizens. At other times the Dinka committee would find slaves in Darfur and Kordofan, but when the group returned to purchase their freedom, the slaves would no longer be there. Even though the government of Sudan has had success in deterring activities of the Dinka Committee, reports from leaders and individuals involved in the Rizeigat community had no involvement in abducting or detaining members of my tribe. The reports also stated objections to the civil war due to injuries and death inflicted by military landmines. One report tells of eleven Rizeigat citizens being killed by a landmine while herding their cattle. This report also said that the Rizeigat community objected the notion of international organizations purchasing abducted slaves and viewed the filmed acts of re-purchasing slaves as a publicity stunt rather than an effort to end the hardships and injustices (Anti-Slavery International, 2001).

In addition to Government enacting policy to limit and prevent the Dinka Committee from rescuing captive slaves, they often were attacked. During the 1990's, the attacks were extended upon members of the International Community, which was helping the Dinka Committee in identifying slaves for rescue.

Difficulties to Ending Slavery

Although slavery is a significant problem that has tainted Sudan since the beginning of the second civil war, there are complexities in determining how to end it. Anti-Slavery International has identified six barriers that significantly increase the difficulty of releasing Dinka and other South Sudanese slaves. The six obstacles are first, definitions of abuse; second, definitions of Sudanese laws; third, the inability to identify abuse as slavery; fourth, the issue of governmental compliancy; fifth, the interest of the victims of slavery, and sixth, military objections (Anti-Slavery International, 2001).

Slavery versus abuse: In Sudan, as in most of the modern world, people don't think of slavery as a modern issue, but rather an issue of ages past. Yet today more than 27-million people are enslaved worldwide (Gordon, 2011) with more than 100,000 enslaved in Sudan during the second Sudanese civil war (PBS, 2003).

Slavery usually begins when one social group or culture views another as weaker or inferior. When this occurs, the first group begins to hate the second group. In Sudan, the government and the northern forces begin to view their

Arabic culture as the only way to live and began to forcefully Islamize the Christian society of South Sudan.

While many nations in the world today are unaware that slavery occurred in the twentieth century, it becomes a challenge to define it. And many nations that do recognize its existence, including the government of Sudan, which fails to regard it as abuse. With the Sudanese government denying that forced labor is slavery, it becomes increasingly difficult for the United Nations and other international organizations to work toward ending it (Anti-Slavery International, 2001).

The definition of Sudanese laws: While the Sudanese government does not recognize the definition of slavery, their legal codes do recognize offences such as forced labor, abduction, kidnapping, unlawful confinement, and unlawful detainment ("Sudanese Law"). Although these terms are identified under Sudanese law, they are rarely enforced and are weak in comparison to the crimes they are punishing. For example, an individual who is accused of abducting a citizen of Southern Sudan at most would receive a maximum sentence of one year in prison, even if the individual they kidnapped was bound in slavery for a decade (Anti-Slavery International, 2001). As long as Sudanese laws remain weak, the problem will remain ultimately unresolved and remain as a potential threat for future generations.

Not labeling abuse as slavery: Due to this view, any trust between my people and the groups that invaded us, causing our hardships to be weakened. This led to future delays in negotiating peace and cooperation, which in turn led to delays within the process of releasing slaves and returning them to their homes. As long as slavery is not defined, any acts of restitution from individuals who abused us and caused us hardships may also be delayed.

The government's denial of slavery: Many reports from other organizations, as well as firsthand accounts of hardships, contradict the government's statements (Anti-Slavery International, 2001; Frontline Fellowship; Human Rights Watch, 2002; PBS, 2003). As long as the government denies that slavery exists within the country's borders, it is difficult for the United Nations and other groups to put an effective, long term end to it.

The interest of the victims who suffered slavery: Although many individuals were taken forcefully into slavery, a percentage of Dinka citizens willfully chose to live among other tribes that contributed militia members hired by the northern government. These people may be mistaken for those taken as slaves during the second civil war when organizations make their efforts to identify slaves to return them to their home community. It is important to identify each person and listen to individual wishes on what and where they wish to go.

The military's objection to releasing the slaves: During the second civil war, it was difficult to find safe passages to rescue slaves and return them home. Although the Sudanese government in its 1999 issued reports on freeing the slaves, it didn't follow through. All the reports did was temporarily please the International community (Anti-Slavery International, 2001).

International Organizations: Recommendations and Solutions

While obstacles stand in the way of ending slavery in Sudan, there have been a number of proposals suggesting feasible solutions. Anti-Slavery International developed a series of eight of them: first, forbid future raids and civilian abductions; second, strengthen the definitions of what constitutes non-permissible activities; third, strengthen the prosecution of offenders; fourth, improve the means in which slaves can return home; fifth, ensure a stronger method to free women who are being forced into marriage; sixth, increase protection for individuals who are responsible for identifying, rescuing, and freeing slaves; seventh, increase governmental resource development for individuals involved in identifying, rescuing, and freeing slaves; eighth, improve governmental involvement in upholding and protecting human rights.

Although raids upon civilian villages ended during the second civil war, there needs to be a stronger method to prevent the same thing happening in the future.

The second solution is for authorities to clearly define what practices are permitted and which ones is not (Anti-Slavery International, 2001). There have to be clear and detailed definitions of what will not be tolerated. This will be more effective at deterring and prosecuting individuals who violated the law than the system of vague and unclear definitions that plagued Sudan during the second civil war. Although this will be difficult and require extensive changes for those in the government who establish laws and legislation, it is a critical step in helping to ensure these tragedies that impacted my people never happen again.

The third solution is to strengthen efforts to prosecute individuals who commit human rights violations, those who abduct or own slaves (Anti-Slavery International, 2001). Once there are clear definitions of what constitutes slavery, the Sudanese government should set specific dates for all slaves to be released and returned to their homes. Once a deadline to release slaves is set, the government should appropriate the resources to ensure the violators are prosecuted in an effective and timely manner.

Even when slaves are freed, they still face having to find safe passage back to their home village (Anti-Slavery International, 2001). They face the risk of encountering unlawful military forces that recapture them. Returning

205

slaves also run the risk of wandering through hostile territories and combat zones. All this undermines the efforts of governmental, domestic, and international organizations efforts to abolish the hardships and tragedies of slavery in Sudan.

The fifth step is to make sure that females are never again forced into relationships. Releasing those forced into a marriage is much more complicated, especially when a woman has children in her home village and children from her slave marriage. Anti-Slavery International recommended "a joint working group from Arabic-speaking and Dinka-speaking groups to make the options clear to the women involved and then allowing them to choose which option to take," (Anti-Slavery International, 2001).

The sixth step is to increase protections for those responsible for tracking down slaves, repurchasing them, and reuniting them with their families. The Dinka Committee and international organizations often do this. However, many of these organizations face strong opposition from local governments, security, and militants. Often, those who oppose releasing slaves conduct violent attacks against those working to end slavery. Thus, the government needs to more aggressively prosecute those committing the crimes. For example, the government should more closely examine governmental employees who own and trade slaves.

The seventh step involves releasing resources to organizations participating in freeing slaves (Anti-Slavery International, 2001). Joe Biden once said, "Do not tell me what you value, show me your budget, and I will tell you what you value," (Good Reads). Most of the organizations, such as the Dinka Committee, that work toward rescuing slaves abducted during the second civil war, receive the majority of their funding from international organizations. Despite denying that slavery exists, the government has many times said they care about those abducted into slavery and will take actions to resolve the issue (Human Rights Watch, 2002). Many times, however, despite such promises, the government has done nothing. It needs to end its empty rhetoric and take action.

The eighth and final step is for the government to issue an announcement about nationally-known and practiced human rights' standards (Anti-Slavery International, 2001). All of the problems related to slavery in Sudan – including violence, murders, rape, forced labor, abductions, and forced marriage – can be summarized as violations of basic human rights known and honored internationally. If slavery is to be ended, those in power need to recognize the violations that occurred and take immediate action to ensure this sort of thing never happens again. As long as basic human rights are ignored in Sudan, problems and hardships will continue.

Current Legal Prosecutions Pending: International Criminal Court

Despite the numerous problems that the government of northern Sudan allowed to occur during the second civil war, organizations such as the International Criminal Court have begun to prosecute individuals responsible for the atrocities committed during the past decades. The organization was established to help "end impunity for the perpetrators of the most serious crimes of concern to the international community" (International Criminal Court). The group operates under the governance of the Rome Statute and is independent of the United Nations, although it is affiliated with the Assembly of State Parties within the UN. That is, it "shall have international legal personality. It shall also have such legal capacity as may be necessary for the exercise of its functions and the fulfillment of its purposes" and "may exercise its functions and powers, as provided in this Statute, on the territory of any State Party and, by special agreement, on the territory of any other State" ("Rome Statute," 1998).

Since the second civil war ended in 2005, many of the government officials that were responsible for the atrocities my people suffered are now being sought by the International Criminal Court. The top officials in northern Sudan that should have been taking actions toward stopping unjust crimes are being placed on trial.

The first official to be is Ahmad Muhammad, former Minister of State for the Interior of the Government if Sudan and Minister of State for Humanitarian Affairs of Sudan. The International Criminal Court issued warrants for his arrest in 2007. The charges included twenty counts of crimes against humanity, specifically for murder, persecution, forcible transfer, rape, inhuman acts, imprisonment or severe deprivation of liberty, and torture. He also is charged with twenty-two war crimes including murder, attacks against the civilian population, destruction of property, and rape pillage (International Criminal Court No. 2). These charges demonstrate the levels of corruption and lack of morals or ethics that reigned during the second civil war. The second official to be charged is Ali Muhammad Ali Abd-Al-Rahman ("Ali Kushayb"). During the second civil war, he was the leader of the Janjaweed and Militia groups responsible for raiding and destroying villages in South Sudan such as the City of Dong. Ali Kushayb currently is charged with fifty counts of criminal behavior including twenty-two counts of crimes against humanity. They too include murder, deportation or forcible transfer of population, imprisonment or other severe deprivation of physical liberty in violation of fundamental rules of international law, torture, persecution, inhumane acts of inflicting serious bodily injury and suffering, and twenty-eight war crimes that consist of violence to life and person, outrage upon personal dignity in particular humiliating and degrading treatment, intentionally directing an attack against a civilian population, pillArab Group International, rape, and destroying or seizing the property (International Criminal Court No. 2).

The third official the group is seeking is Omar Hassan Ahmad al-Bashir, president of the Republic of Sudan since October 16, 1993, who has ten charges being brought against him. They are five counts of crimes against humanity including murder, extermination, forcible transfer, torture, and rape, as well as two counts of war crimes. These involve intentionally directing attacks against a civilian population or against individual civilians not taking part in hostilities, and three counts of genocide including (International Criminal Court, #2).

The fourth government official under investigation is Bahar Idriss Abu Garda. Former Chairman and General Coordinator of Military Operations of the United Resistance Front during the second civil war, he was questioned about three possible war crimes including murder, whether committed or attempted, directing attacks against personnel, installations, material, units, or vehicles involved in a peacekeeping mission. In 2010, at a pre-trial hearing these charges were not confirmed. However, the International Criminal Court may attempt to bring them forward again if additional evidence is obtained (International Criminal Court No. 2).

The fifth official is Abdel Raheem Muhammad Hussein, who is Sudan's Minister of National Defense. He also was Sudan's former Minister of the Interior and has previous experience working as the president's special representative in Darfur. Hussein's warrant is currently pending as of March 1, 2012. It is based on thirteen counts of individual responsibility for criminal activity. They consist of seven counts of crimes against humanity including persecution, murder, forcible transfer, rape, inhumane acts, and imprisonment or severe deprivation of liberty, and torture. In addition, he is charged with six counts of war crimes including murder, attacks against a civilian population, destruction of property, rape, and outrage upon personal dignity (International Criminal Court No. 2).

On March 7, 2011, the International Criminal Court confirmed charges against two men cooperating in committing three war crimes. Their names are Abdallah Banda Abakaer Nourain, the Command-in-Chief of Justice and Equality Movement Collective-Leadership within the United Resistance Front, and Saleh Mohammed Jerbo Jamus, former Chief of Staff of the Southern Liberation Army-Unity, and official within the Justice and Equity Movement. Nourain and Jamus were charged with violence to life, whether committed or attempted; intentionally directing attacks against personnel, installations, material units, or vehicles involved in a peacekeeping mission (International Criminal Court No. 2).

Causes of War: Oil in Sudan

The discovery of oil in Sudan, during the 1970's, fueled the fire of conflict that had been raging for decades. This discovery added another dimension to the already existing conflict: a dimension of valuable economic resources. Upon the discovery, northern officials became interested in figuring out how to obtain this precious resource. The majority of the oil fields are located in Southern Sudan on lands that belong to my tribe and others, such as the Nuer. Thus, the northern government made plans to clear the land (Derks, and Romer, 2008).

Beginning in 1983, President Nimeiri began to equip and train northern soldiers to invade Southern Sudan. In addition to northern soldiers coming to clear the land for oil, Nimeiri began to recruit members of the Nuer tribe to help. The soldiers attacked the villages, driving them out and leaving the land clear so oil wells could be drilled. Attacks such as these are what forced many boys, including myself, to march across Sudan into Ethiopia.

By 1986, governmental forces from the north took possession of most of the western upper Nile River (Derks and Romer, 2008). At this point the government was in talks about a possible peaceful settlement that would end any future and potential bloodshed. However, one day before legislation would have been passed to suspend Sharia law, the National Islamic Front, led by northern general Omar al-Bashir, the future president of Sudan, initiated a revolt. So instead of Sharia law being suspended, the revolt resulted in increased persecution and an increased call for the north to wage jihad upon the south, a future occupation of Osama Bin-Laden in Sudan during the 1990's, and for a ban of all non-Arabic, non-Islamic political parties.

In 1997, the government, which now owned a larger number of oil fields, needed to derive a way to attract foreign investment. So the government began to draw up agreements to establish peace between various political groups, especially in regions that had many oil fields. While these agreements argued for peace in oil-heavy regions, this never came about. The government armed various Nuer tribes with weapons and equipment and sent them off to fight other African tribes (Derks and Romer, 2008). When foreign investors asked about such conflicts, the government said this was a result of naturally occurring conflict between local tribes, something the investors shouldn't worry about. To make the situation worse the government did not implement any peace agreements. Instead, it sent additional forces into the areas where oil fields were located.

Two years later, in 1999, the first oil pipeline was complete and oil production could begin. Government profits from the sale of oil went to re-investing in efforts to take over South Sudan. This created even more imbalance. Those hardest hit were civilians in villages such as Dong, which was located near the oil fields. Thousands of civilians would continue to be killed, looted, taken into slavery, and displaced.

Importance of Oil: Economic Overview

The conflict resulted in the deaths of hundreds of thousands of people and the displacement of millions of others including myself. The conflict is deeply tied into the country's current macroeconomic situation. Oil is Sudan's leading export and accounts for 92 percent of all exports. Growth in real Gross Domestic Product since oil production began in the late 1990's has expanded from 6.1 percent in 2001 to 11.2 percent in 2007. Gross Domestic Product has more than tripled between 2001 and 2007. Gross National Product per Capita has tripled, as well, since oil production began, starting at $374 in 2001 up to $1,182 in 2007 (IMF Executive Board, 2007). With Sudan in a state of post-conflict, the country currently stands better than a lot of other post-war nations. For example, Sudan has a Gross Domestic Product Per Capita thirty-five times greater than that of Afghanistan.

Although oil is the greatest contribution toward the Sudanese economy, it employs only a small percentage of the workforce. Only about four percent of the population contributes directly to the production of oil. Another eight percent supports the oil industry by building "pipelines, refineries, roads, power stations, and dams," (Bank Audi Sal, 2007).

Despite the vast increases in wealth the investments have brought into Sudan, my tribe and the rest of South Sudan received little in benefits promised to us from the oil companies and government agreements. Although better off than other post-conflict regions, Sudan has a Gross Domestic Product that is approximately only fifty percent of the average for an African state (Derks, and Romer, 2008). Southern Sudan also suffers from extreme poverty resulting from the destructive conflict over oil.

Comprehensive Peace Agreement Oil Companies

The Sudanese oil industry has investments from businesses all over the world, primarily from parts of Asia, the Middle East, and Europe.

The country has key ties to the nations of China, Malaysia, and India. In 2005, China was Sudan's top destination for oil exports. In that year alone, China received seventy-one percent of Sudan's total exports or seven to eight percent of their total oil imports from Sudan (Derks and Romer, 2008). Sudan also receives imports from China including, in 2005, approximately eighty-three million dollars' worth of weapons and arms (Amnesty International, 2007). Malaysia has invested about a fourth as much as China. India too has business investments that include the importation of 75,000 barrels of oil per day and investment projects costing easily over half a billion dollars (Sudan Tribune, 2006).

These Asians promote destruction and have an adverse impact upon South Sudan. According to 1stTimothy 6:10: "[f]or the love of money is the root of all evil." Although the United States, parts of Europe, and the United Nations imposed economic sanctions and embargos upon Sudan in an attempt to protect and deter the violence and injustices caused by the northern Sudanese government during the second Sudanese civil war, the actions taken on behalf of Asian industries and governments negate the positive impacts taken by western government to help deter and stop the humanitarian injustices that occurred in South Sudan.

Oil Companies: Early Days and Chevron

The exploration for oil in Sudan first began in the early part of the twentieth century, but didn't develop into anything significant until a half century later (*Understanding Sudan*, 2009). The first major operation began in the 1950's by the Italian company Arab Group International, (Azienda Generale Italiana Petroli), with over half the corporation belonging to the Italian Department of Treasury. The company drilled six wells (Derks, and Romer, 2008) in the Northeast, offshore in the Red Sea. Other European and American companies began to invest in Sudan around the same time. These include Oceanic Oil Company, Total, Texas Eastern, Union Texas, and Chevron. However, these investments remained extremely small and produced minimal results.

Two decades later, more extensive investments were made into Sudan, resulting in greater quantities of oil being discovered during the 1970's after the first Sudanese Civil War. During this time, American companies such as Chevron and Shell (Derks and Romer, 2008) invested hundreds of millions of dollars into surveying, drilling, and installing other infrastructure related to oil production. These investments began in 1974 when Chevron received permission to begin searching for oil. They were in agreement with the Shell (Sudan) Development Company, Ltd. by taking a 25 percent interest in Chevron's operations. The searches resulted in the discovery of oil, in 1978, in the Muglad Basin, and the Western Upper Nile River region. Three years later, Chevron had more success in locating potential fields to harvest. These were located east of the White Nile River, in a region controlled by my people, called Adar Yale, located in the Melut Basin region (Derks and Romer, 2008).

With Chevron successfully finding oil across the Sudan, the company found much more oil in Heglig, a region located in territory that belonged to the Nuer tribe. Soon the company began to develop the area for drilling wells. (Derks and Romer, 2008).

Thereafter, Sudan began to open up concessions to other international companies. In 1982, the government gave a concession of 118km² to the French-Belgium company Total (Derks and Romer, 2008). While Chevron was required to pay a 25 percent fee to the government, Total was exempt from such exploitations (*Understanding Sudan*, 2009).

By the mid-1980's, conflict broke out between northern and southern Sudan, forcing Chevron to reconsider its business operations in the country. In 1983, when the civil war began, Chevron suspended its operations. One year later, Chevron officially stopped operations when three employees died as a result of the conflict. They were killed by a group called Anyanya II (Derks and Romer, 2008; *Understanding Sudan*, 2009). Anyanya II consisted of members of the Nuer tribe and existed to resist governmental control. Anyanya II ended up dissolving with portions absorbed into the Sudan's Peoples' Liberation Army. After the three deaths, Chevron demanded the presence of more security. However, during the following years, Chevron became displeased by the increasing amount of bloodshed occurring around its operations. By 1988, the company withdrew all operations in the Bentiu and Unity provinces, resulting in a billion dollar loss to Chevron.

Oil Companies Intermediaries and Concorp

Immediately following Chevron's withdrawal, oil production came to a halt, even though Sudanese president, Jafar Nimeiri, attempted to reconstruct political boundaries in order to re-locate many of the oil fields to northern providences. At the time, blueprints were being drafted for the first oil pipeline, which was to run through the northern regions toward the Red Sea. The blueprints would help establish a reason for further funding of northern Sudanese infrastructure (*Understanding Sudan*, 2009).

By 1990, the oil fields Chevron had abandoned were divided up into smaller operating regions called Blocks. In 1992, the government awarded Blocks three and seven, located along the Melut Basin, to the Gulf Petroleum Corporation-Sudan (Derks and Romer, 2008). In October of 1996, the company re-opened the abandoned oil drills and continued to build and improve roadways running from the Melut Basin to the Red Sea. Oil from the re-opened drills was produced at a rate of 5,000 barrels per day in 1996 and doubled to 10,000 barrels per day in 1998. Oil from these drills was shipped along the newly built roads to the Red Sea.

Portions of Chevron were also sold to Concorp International, "owned by a senior member of the National Islamic Front, with no experience in oil production" (*Understanding Sudan*, 2009). Although formed in 1976, the group had experience in constructing buildings, roads, bridges, and schools. This sale was controversial with individuals in political parties, such as the Umma party, stating that the sale put additional power into the hands of the International Islamic Front. The officials involved in the purchase included Osman Abdel Wahab Sulaiman, the Sudanese Minister of Oil, as well as businessmen and financial managers associated with the Faisal Islamic Bank. These included Sheikh Abd-al Basri, Eltayeb el-Nus, and Osman Khalid Mudawi. The President of Concorp, who purchased the oil fields, was Mohammed Abdullah Jar el-Nabi from Darfur. Jar el-Nabi was an early member of the Sudanese Muslim Brotherhood and had been a member of the Sudanese parliament during the mid-1980's. Some Chevron employees began work for Concorp, including general manager Abdelatif Widatalla. Although Chevron had invested billions of dollars in oil operations in Sudan, it sold its operations for only twenty-five million dollars ("Soil and Oil," page 9-10, 2006).

During this time, production remained very low with an average of between 2,000 and 3,000 barrels per day, a small fraction of what other companies were producing in other Blocks ("Understanding Sudan," 2009).

By August of 1993, Concorp resold its rights to oil production back to the Sudanese Government. However, the company continued to remain a small player in the industry. On June 19, 1995, Concorp purchased a small fraction of the Gulf Petroleum Company and opened a refinery in the South (*Soil and Oil*, page 11, 2006). At the same time Concorp president el-Nabi continued to pursue other business investments in Sudan and Uganda. On occasion, he tried to effect peace agreements between the Sudanese government and the Sudan's Peoples' Liberation Army and their allies (*Soil and Oil*, page 11, 2006). Despite these, el-Nabi was associated with smuggling weapons to al Qaeda in the late 1990's for the purpose of attacking United States embassies in eastern Africa (*Soil and Oil*, page 11, 2006; United States vs. Osama bin-Laden, 2001).

Oil Companies: Canadian Involvement

Soon after ConCorp sold the rights to the government, they were re-sold to a small Canadian company. State Petroleum of Vancouver was incorporated in November of 1991 after the owner Lutfur Rahman Khan, originally from Pakistan, took a trip to Sudan to find a means to enter into the oil industry. Khan signed an agreement with the government to allow him access to the oil fields in exchange for sharing profits with the government. Many questions were raised about how a small, newly-formed oil company from Canada acquired access to the Sudanese oil fields (*Soil and Oil*, 2006). However, almost immediately afterward, the company sold its holdings to another Canadian company called Arakis Energy Corporation, owned by J. Terry Alexander (*Understanding Sudan*, 2009).

While Blocks three and seven were awarded to the Gulf Petroleum Corporation, in 1992 and 1993 Blocks one, two, and four went to the Canadian company. The purchase raised controversy about unethical activities. Alexander was an investor in the Vancouver Stock Exchange and had traded commodities and pharmaceuticals since the mid 1960's. Thus, it was no surprise that the trade of oil fields in Sudan occurred on the Vancouver Stock Exchange, historically known for unethical and illicit activities. In a 1989 issue of *Forbes* magazine, the stock exchange was declared the "Scum Capitol of the World" and was responsible for "polluting much of the civilized world" (Queenan, 1989).

In 1992, Alexander began to seek funding for Arakis Energy's operations in Sudan through the International Finance Corporation. He discovered, however, that this would be too difficult. (*Tiny, little-known Arakis*, 1993). Subsequently, he held fundraisers in which shares were traded privately rather than on the public exchange. He used offshore locations in the British Virgin Islands and Liechtenstein to avoid paying taxes. Once he had acquired the stock he wanted, he hid it within another company's books and shifted it back onto the publicly traded exchange (*Soil and Oil*, page 14-15, 2009). Alexander's trading schemes failed at one point, resulting in regulatory fines totaling $1.2 million dollars. Although he was fined for illicit activities, he still received significant profits through his offshore trades. Alexander's company forged alliances with Sudanese officials operating in the National Islamic Front.

Soon after transferring the right of oil operations from the State Petroleum of Vancouver to the Arakis Energy Corporation, the Sudanese Government, headed by the National Islamic Front, launched additional "expulsion" campaigns into the Heglig and Unity Regions. Hired militias led the attacks in order to clear land for oil production. This occurred during the dry seasons of 1992 and 1993 (*Understanding Sudan*, 2009).

Between 1992 and 1996, the Arakis Energy Corporation discovered many new oil fields located in their three blocks. However, the company was unable to raise enough funds to pursue the construction required to harvest the newly found oil (Derks and Romer, 2008). Oil production remained relatively low. The average production in Blocks controlled by Arakis was only 3,200 barrels per day (*Understanding Sudan*, 2009). Arakis Energy Corporation sought people willing to invest into their operations.

In 1994, Arakis Energy began to contract trucking and shipping services with the Regions Internal Investment Company, a subsidiary of the Arab Group International. The company is an international business group located in Saudi Arabia and is the parent company to the Regions Internal Investment Company. Heading the company was Saudi

Arabian Prince Sultan Bin Saud Bin Abdullah Al Saud. Arakis Energy was extremely impressed and satisfied with the services they had received from the Regions Internal Investment Company and so began to inquire about additional involvement in the company's operations. In December of 1994, the two companies discussed having Arab Group International invest additional capital in Sudanese oil operations (*Soil and Oil*, page 16, 2009).

In 1995, negotiations between Arakis and Arab Group International were made public. Arakis announced publically that Arab Group International would be providing financial capital to its operations. The announcement caused Arakis to soar in value on the NASDAQ stock exchange (*Understanding Sudan*, 2009). Before the public announcement in February of 1995, a share of Arakis was valued just under five Canadian dollars. By July, the value had increased by approximately 700 percent to thirty-three Canadian dollars. The company's total worth had grown to just under $1.2 billion dollars (*Soil and Oil*, page 17, 2006).

By August 1995, political changes began to occur within the Saudi Arabian government. Questions began to arise about the legitimacy of the royal family's involvement in Arab Group International. Many officials in the Saudi Arabian government were replaced, including the Saudi Oil Minister Hisham Nazir, whohad major involvement in the Arab Group International's financial activities (*Soil and Oil*, page 17, 2006). As a result of the changes and issues arising in Saudi Arabia, Arab Group International's investments into Arakis' Sudanese oil operations fell through. By the end of 1995 Arakis Energy Corporation was removed from the Vancouver Exchange and was officially delisted from the NASDAQ stock exchange (*Understanding Sudan*, 2009). Arakis was now desperate to find new investors.

In addition to financial pressures being placed on Arakis, due to its inability to find adequate investments, political and human rights pressures began to affect the company, as well. International organizations including the Inter-Church Collation on Africa said in a press release that the group was concerned that investments from Arakis and other oil companies would help fund the Sudanese Government. "With Arakis investment dollars, the Sudanese regime will receive huge amounts of money, which can be used to prolong the country's devastating civil war and maintain its repressive state security apparatus" (Baines, 1995). Despite the atrocities and human rights violations occurring in Sudan, Arakis CEO Alexander downplayed the conflict and continued to support the government. He stated that "there are brief skirmished... but it is mostly a civil dispute within different tribes in the south and they vie for domination, feeding grounds, or better agricultural area. In any case, it does not involve our project" (Baines, 1995). Alexander was also recorded as stating "we don't have an ideological vision of Sudan; we are only an oil company" (Baines, 1995). The pressures from international human rights organization only further added to Arakis' mission of seeking additional investments in its Sudanese operations.

While Arakis was seeking new investment opportunities and responding to pressure from the International Community, the government used this opportunity to launch additional campaigns into oil fields in Southern Sudan in an attempt to clear out additional land for future investments. By October of 1996, the government and the Murahaleen launched more attacks in the regions north of Heglig and the western upper Nile River (*Soil and Oil*, page 19, 2006). These attacks displaced thousands of residents.

Oil Companies: Greater Nile Petroleum Operating Company

In November of 1996, Arakis sold 75 percent of its ownership in Sudanese operations to a group called the Greater Nile Petroleum Operating Company, which consisted of companies owned by the governments of Sudan, China, and Malaysia. The company retained 25 percent (Derks and Romer, 2008). The Greater Nile Petroleum Operating Company was owned 25 percent by the Arakis Energy Corporation from Canada, 40 percent by the China National Petroleum Corporation, 30 percent by Petronas from Malaysia, and 5 percent by the Sudan National Petroleum Company (Pipeline partners,). The company's activities led to investments worth multiple billions of dollars. The new foreign investors from China and Malaysia bankrolled all required investments of infrastructure (*Soil and Oil*, page 19, 2006). This, in part, led to the first major production of oil in Sudan.

By March of 1997, Greater Nile Petroleum began building the first major oil pipeline in Sudan. It would run from the fields in Southern Sudan outward toward the Red Sea where oil could be easily exported. The pipeline eventually stretched 1540km or approximately 957 miles (Derks and Romer, 2008).

Although Arakis Energy owned a fourth of the newly-formed company, Alexander was unable to fulfill the obligations agreed upon in negotiations. Operations were transferred to Talisman Energy, another Canadian company (*Understanding Sudan*, 2009).

Between February of 1997 and January of 1998, contracts were drafted and awarded to suppliers to use the pipeline. They were issued to Chinese, Malaysian, and European companies. The first major contract went to the China Petroleum Engineer and Construction Company, a subsidiary of the China National Petroleum Company, to begin work on the development of oil fields located within the Heglig ("Sudan Consortium," 1997). The company spent over a billion dollars to construct the pipeline. Greater Nile, in addition to using Chinese and Malaysian companies, purchased engines and pumps from Rolls Royce and Weir Pumps in the United Kingdom (*Soil and Oil*, page 21, 2006).

The first two thousand workers from China arrived in Sudan on May 1, 1998. Around this time the Greater Nile Petroleum Operating Company began to partner with the Sudanese firm DAL Engineering, owned by Osama Daoud Abdel Latif (*Soil and Oil*, page 21, 2006; Stokes, 1998).

In August of 1999, the oil pipeline was finally completed, and the first 600,000 barrels of oil were loaded onto shipping boats on the Red Sea to be sent to refineries in the Far East (Derks and Romer, 2008; *Soil and Oil*, page 21, 2006). Sudanese president Bashir and Iraqi Oil Minister Hasan al-Turabi attended the oil celebratory ceremonies.

Despite the celebrations, the Sudanese military began another offensive in a 100 km radius surrounding the Heglig oil fields. As had happened previously, attacks were carried out with bombardments, helicopter gunships, artillery, and tanks. In response, Sudan's People Liberation Army began a series of attacks on the new pipeline. John Garang, a member of the group, officially declared the pipeline an official military target (*Understanding Sudan*, 2008). On September 20, 1999, a section of the oil pipeline was attacked and damaged, approximately 350 km north of Khartoum(*Soil and Oil*,page 21-22, 2006).

In response, the Sudanese Interior Ministry deployed three thousand law enforcement officers along the pipeline, as well as providing military support. This involved contracting militia groups, including the SSDF under the control of Riek Machar, the al Himmat al Bitrol militia, the al

Fatih al Mubin militia, a sub-group within the Peoples Defense Force called the Protectors of the Oil Brigade, and forces controlled by Paulino Matiep (*Soil and Oil*, page 21-22, 2006). Many of the militias were sponsored by President Bashir, Vice President Ali Osman Taha, and "[A] Chinese oil company also had contracted with the Sudanese government to ensure the security of its operations" (Amenity International; "Soil and oil," page 22, 2006).

In addition to contracting with the government of Sudan to acquire additional military forces to defend the oil fields and pipeline, the Greater Nile Petroleum Operating Company hired its own private military and security personnel. It was reported there was a close working relationships between the government and the private security forces (Harker, 2000).

The Coalition for International Justice found that "those in charge of security operations are the same as those tasked with community development project. The manager of security operations for the oil fields and pipeline also oversees healthcare, education capacity development, and freshwater supply. However, these projects have little or no oversight," (*Soil and Oil*, page 23, 2006).

In 2000, agreements between the Greater Nile Petroleum Operating Company and the government allowed security and military forces to use refueling stations for defensive military purposes. These refueling stations were originally intended for business use to fuel vehicles related to oil production.

In 2000, Talisman Energy addressed serious problems that were occurring at the refueling stations. The company defined defensive security support that which "assists those forces legitimately deployed within the concession area to protect personnel and property in which, in achieving those objectives, uses a proportionate level of force" and defined offensive activity in this report as "anything outside the parameters defined as defensive" (Talisman Energy: Corporate, 2000). The firm issued reports that "the government was using the infrastructure – e.g. helicopter landing pads – for reasons it could not determine were defensive" (*Understanding Sudan*, 2009). Specifically, in 2000, Talisman found four documented instances in which "helicopters and planes landed on the airstrip for reasons we could not determine were related to oil field security" (Talisman Energy: Corporate, 2000).

While Talisman Energy was generating reports regarding social issues that had been occurring within Sudan, other investors and members of the Greater Nile Petroleum Operating Company continued turning a blind eye to these occurrences and supported future destruction. The government's cut from Greater Nile helped support the effort against the Sudan's People Liberation Army. China, which owned 40 percent of Greater Nile, continued to benefit from Sudanese oil in more ways than their share of profits. China happened to be the largest supplier of military weapons and equipment to the government of Sudan, which was taking the currency earned from the sale of oil to purchase these weapons. Between 2000 and 2002, following the increased profits from oil production in Sudan, the government increased its fleet of helicopter gunships from six in 2000 to twenty-two in 2002 (*Understanding Sudan*, 2009). In 2002, the government continued to use military forces to remove civilians from regions surrounding the Greater Nile oil fields. The attacks in 2002 were carried out by helicopters purchased from Chinese weapons suppliers (*Soil and Oil*, page 24, 2006; *Understanding Sudan*, 2009).

Russia also supplied some of the helicopter gunships, which would be used up through the Darfur conflicts during the following decade (*Soil and Oil*, page 24, 2006).

When it became widely known that the government was using infrastructure and oil profits to support and prolong the civil war, many international human rights' organizations put pressure on members of Greater Nile, specifically Talisman Energy. Although the dominant partner in Greater Nile, the Chinese National Petroleum Company, was setting the agenda and held the closest connections to the government. Talisman Energy took the fall and drew attention from the international community for two reasons. First, they took an adversarial in opposing the activities occurring in Sudan and also took stand for corporate social responsibility. Second, Talisman Energy was the only participating company that was privately owned. All others were para-statal, or governmentally owned (*Soil and Oil*, page 27, 2006).

Outside groups wanted reinvestment of profits to be used to improve life for the country's civilians. Between 2001 and 2002, Talisman Energy spent approximately six million in community development projects. However, this investment was viewed as extremely small and insufficient in helping rebuild and aid portions of South Sudan that had been ravaged by the civil war and oil production. The six million was only one percent of Talisman Energy's total revenue during those two years. To make matters worse the six million was invested into community developed in northern Sudan instead of in the south where it was desperately needed (*Understanding Sudan*, 2009).

In 2001, pressures from international organizations continued against Talisman Energy. As a result, the company's Energy Chief Executive Officer Dr. James Buckee began to search for someone to purchase Talisman Energy's share of Greater Nile's operations. By November of 2002, Talisman signed a contract with Oil and Natural Gas Corporation Ltd., a state-owned company from India. The firm would end up spending $758 million dollars for the right to operate in Sudan. After expenses, Talisman would walk away with two hundred million dollars in profits (Talisman Sells, 2002). After Talisman sold its operations, China National Petroleum Corporation, the Chinese parastatal, Petronas, and the new Oil and Natural Gas Corporation Ltd. would now account for over ninety percent of all Sudanese oil production.

In 2003, the Chinese National Petroleum Company discovered two new oil fields located in Blocks three and seven. During 2003, the oil production from the new fields would result in a jump to 270,000 barrels of oil per day and eventually climb to 304,000 barrels by 2004 (Derks and Romer, 2008).

While the oil companies that had millions of dollars invested in Sudanese oil production were becoming wealthy, tribes suffered. The government of Northern Sudan used their military to wreak havoc upon our lands. They invaded villages, killing thousands, raping the women, taking young boys into slavery, and forcing many to flee thousands of miles across the rugged and dangerous African terrain to safety. The Peoples Armed Forces was ordered to "[g]uard the oil... and work for oil exploration and roads. Also to relocate all civilians to inside towns and evacuation of all other forces from the routes leading to" (Talisman Court). Rather than taking steps toward ending people's hardships, oil companies began to request security from the Peoples Armed Forces, and in some instances even consulted for the Peoples Armed Forces by providing logistical support on military offenses (Derks and Romer, 2008).

Decades after the massacre, the oil companies have done nothing to compensate the citizens of the south. Being overlooked in such a way continues to build animosity and distrust between the tribes of South Sudan and the government forces in Northern Sudan.

BIBLIOGRAPHY

(2004). *Protocol between the government of Sudan (gos) and the Sudan'sPeople's Liberation Army/Movement (SPLA/M) on the resolution of abyei conflict*

Amnesty International, Sudan: arms continuing to fuel serious human rights violations in Darfur. 8 May 2007.

Anti-slavery.(n.d.).*Slavery in Sudan*. Retrieved from http://www.antislavery.org/english/what_we_do/antislavery_international_today/award/2006_award_winner/slavery

Anti-slavery, 2.(n.d.).*Bonded labour*. Retrieved from http://www.antislavery.org/english/slavery_today/bonded_labour.aspx

Anti-Slavery International. (2001). Is there still slavery in sudan.*Antislavery.org*, Retrieved from http://www.antislavery.org/includes/documents/cm_docs/2009/i/isthereslaveryinsudanreport.pdf

Arbitration agreement between the government of Sudan and the Sudan people's liberation movement/army on delimiting abyei area. (2008, July 7). Retrieved from http://www.pca-cpa.org/showfile.asp?fil_id=1117

Asim El-Moghraby, in: ECOS, Oil and the Future of Sudan, Report of a Conference in Juba, 1-2 November 2006, p. 33.

Baines, David, (1995): "Arakis put profits before lives, groups changes: BAINES: 'Only a facade for NIF," *Vancouver Sun*, 25 July 1995

Bank Audi Sal, Sudan Economic Report. Beirut, December 2006 (30 August 2007).

BBC.No. 1 (n.d.).*The History of Africa Islam.* Retrieved from http://www.bbc.co.uk/worldservice/africa/features/storyof africa/7chapter3.shtml

BBC.No. 2 (n.d.).*The History of Africa: Africa and Europe.* Retrieved from http://www.bbc.co.uk/worldservice/africa/features/storyof africa/11chapter5.shtml

Beshir, M. O. (1968).*The Southern Sudan: Background to Conflict.* (p. 11). London: Hurst.

Burr, M. (1998). Quantifying genocide in southern Sudan and the Nuba Mountains, 1983-1998.*Washington, D.C.: U.S. Committee for Refugees,*

Coalition for International Justice, (2006).*Soil and Oil: Dirty business in Sudan.* Retrieved from website: http://sudan.uconn.edu/CIJ-Soil_and_Oil_Dirty_Business_in_Sudan_2006.pdf

Crook, J. R. (2009). Abyei arbitration – final award.*American Society of International Law,13*(15), Retrieved from http://www.asil.org/files/insight090916pdf.pdf

Derks, A., & Romer, E. (2008). Sudan: Whose old? Sudan's old industry.*Fatal Transactions*

ECOS, Oil and the Future of Sudan, Report of a Conference in Juba, 1-2 November 2006, p. 21.

Eibner, J. (1999). My Career Redeeming Slaves.*Middle East Quarterly,4*(4), 3-16. Retrieved from http://www.meforum.org/449/my-career-redeeming-slaves

Fleuhr-Lobban, C. (1990). Islamization in Sudan: A critical assessment.*Middle East Quarterly,*

Freedom House.(n.d.).*Fact-finding report confirms Sudan slavery.* Retrieved from http://www.freedomhouse.org/article/factfinding-report-confirms-sudan-slavery?

Frontline Fellowship.(n.d.).*Islamic slave trade exposed*. Retrieved from
http://www.aggressivechristianity.net/islam/sudan2.htm

Global Security.(2012).*Sudan-first civil war*. Retrieved from
http://www.globalsecurity.org/military/world/war/sudan-civil-war1.htm

Good Reads. (n.d.).*Joe Bidenquote*. Retrieved from
http://www.goodreads.com/quotes/10478-don-t-tell-me-what-you-value-show-me-your-budget

Gordon, S. (2011, Jan 11).*Human trafficking awareness day: 27 million people are enslaved right now*. Retrieved from
http://blog.causes.com/2011/01/human-trafficking-awareness-day-27-million-people-are-enslaved-right-now/

Harker (2000).Talisman Corporate Social Responsibility Report 2001.

Henderson, K. K. D. (1965).*Sudan Republic*. (p. 162). London: Ernest Benn.

Human Rights Watch. (2002, March).*Slavery and slave redemption in the Sudan: Human rights watch backgrounder*. Retrieved from

IMF Executive Board Concludes 2007 Article IV Consultation with Sudan, Public Information Notice (PIN) No. 07/121, October 3, 2007,
http://www.imf.org/external/np/sec/pn/2007/pn07121.htm.

International Criminal Court.(n.d.).*About the court*. Retrieved from http://www.icc-cpi.int/Menus/ICC/About the Court/

International Criminal Court, No. 2.(n.d.).*Darfur, Sudan*. Retrieved from http://www.icc-cpi.int/Menus/ICC/Situations and Cases/Situations/Situation ICC 0205/

Interviews with chiefs in Northern Upper Nile, April 2005.

Katendeko, F. (2003, Sept. 09).*Sudan's 50 year war*. Retrieved from http://www.monitor.upeace.org/archive.cfm?id_article=87

Kendall, T. (n.d.).*Black kingdoms of the Nile*. Retrieved from http://www.pbs.org/wonders/Episodes/Epi1/nile_2.htm

Labb, T. (2004, Jan 11). A legacy hidden in plain sight Iraqis of African descent are a largely overlooked link to slavery.*Washington Post*. Retrieved from http://www.washingtonpost.com/ac2/wp-dyn?pagename=article&contentId=A6645-2004Jan10¬Found=true

Lewis, B. (1996).*The Middle East, 2,000 years of history from the rise of Christianity to the present day*. (p. 209). London: Phoenix Giant.

Lokichoggio. (1999). apid assessment report, rapid assessment of affected locations in twic, aweil east, aweil west and wau counties, march 13 and 25, 1999.*UNICEF/OLS Rapid Assessment Team*, (Apr.),

Michalowski, K., "The Spreading of Christianity in Nubia," p.338

Part XVI of the Penal Code. (n.d.).*Sudanese law*(Articles 162-165)

PBS. (2003, Sept 23).*Dying to leave: Human trafficking*. Retrieved from http://www.pbs.org/wnet/wideangle/episodes/dying-to-leave/human-trafficking-worldwide/sudan/1460/

Pipeline partners.(n.d.). Retrieved from http://www.sudanupdate.org/REPORTS/Oil/17cos.html

Queenan, J. (1989, May 29). Scum capitol of the world.*ForbesMArab Group Internationalzine*, 132.

Rubin, M. (2001, Dec. 21).*Wall Street Journal*

Salih, A. (n.d.).*The history of Africa Islam*. Retrieved from http://www.bbc.co.uk/worldservice/africa/features/storyof africa/7chapter3.shtml

Shinnie, P.L.,*Ancient Nubia*(London: Kegan Paul International, 1996)

Shanmugaratnam, N. (n.d.).*Post-war development and the land question in south Sudan.* Informally published manuscript, Department of International Environment & Development Studies, Noragric Norwegian University of Life Sciences , Noragric Norwegian University of Life Sciences, Aas, Norway. Retrieved from http://www.umb.no/statisk/noragric/publications/shan_le ctures/shan_southsudan_landquestion.pdf

Spaulding, J. (1995). Medieval Christian Nubia and the Islamic world: a reconsideration of the Baqttreaty. *International Journal of African Historical Studies,28*(3), 577.

Stokes, Paul: "Weir Lands 20m Pound Pipeline Contract," *The Scotsman,* 19 February 1998

"Story of an Immigrant."(123HelpMe.com. 14 Oct 2015)

Sudan consortium awards CPECC Contract for the Development of the Heglig Fields; *Middle East Economic Survey,* 10 February 1997

Sudan: History. In (2007).*The Columbia Electronic Encyclopedia*(6 ed.). Columbia University Press.

Sudan's slaves, adding to the list of crimes in Darfur. 2008.*Wall Street Journal.* Retrieved from http://online.wsj.com/article/SB123051162714738469.html

Sudan Tribune, Sudan, India sign agreement on agricultural researches, 13 June 2006.

Sudan Update.(n.d.).*Sudan-slavery briefing.* Retrieved from http://www.sudanupdate.org/REPORTS/Slavery/slave.htm

Talisman court case documents, found in US court district of Manhattan

Talisman Energy: Corporate Social Responsibility Report 2000

Talisman Sells Sudan Assets to ONGY Videsh, *Middle East Economic Survey*,4 November 2002

Tiny, little-know Arakis seeking new financing. (1993, Jan. 23).*Platt's Oilgram News*

Understanding Sudan: A teaching and learning resource. (2009). Retrieved from http://understandingsudan.org/oil/OilResources/L2FS2-HistoryofOilinSudan.pdf

United Nations, (1998).*Rome Statute*(Treaty Series, vol. 2187, No. 38544). Retrieved from website: http://www.icc-cpi.int/NR/rdonlyres/ADD16852-AEE9-4757-ABE7-9CDC7CF02886/283503/RomeStatutEng1.pdf

United States v. Osama Bin Laden, S(7)98 Cr.1023(LBS), 2001 U.S. Dist. LEXIS 15484 (S.D.N.Y.2001), (1998 Embassy bombing trial), transcript, day 2, 6 February 2001.

Vantini, G. (1981).*Christianity in the Sudan.* (pp. 65-67). Bologna.

Yasin , A. M. O. (1999, April).*Statement by Ali Mohamed Osman Yasin, minister of justice and attorney general, republic of Sudan, to the fifty-fifth session of the United Nations commission on human rights.* Geneva.

FURTHER READING

Africa Watch. Sudan: New Islamic Penal Code Violates Basic Human
Rights. New York, April 1991.

An-Na''im, Abdullahi and Peter Kok. Fundamentalism and Militarism: A Report on the Root Causes of Human Rights Violations in The Sudan. New York: The Fund for Peace, 1991.

Badri, Dina. "Religion and Peace in Sudan: Inter-religious Dialogue and Peaceful Coexistence," Ahfad Journal 21.1(2004): 41-52.

Brown, Stuart. Seeking an Open Society: Interfaith Relations and Dialogue in Sudan Today. Nairobi, Kenya: Paulines Publications Africa, 1997.

Deng, Francis. War of Visions: Conflicting Identities in the Sudan. Washington, DC: Brookings Institute, 1995.

The Economist. "Jihad." August 7, 1993.
Esposito, John (ed.). Islam in Transition. Oxford: Oxford University Press, 1982.

Esposito, John (ed.). Voices of Resurgent Islam. Oxford: Oxford University Pr ess, 1983.

Hasan, Yusuf Fadl & Richard Gray. Religion and Conflict in Sudan: Papers from an International Conference at Yale, May 1999.

Nairobi: Paulines Publications Africa, 2002.

Hertzke, Alan D. Freeing God's Children: The Unlikely Alliance for Global Human Rights. New York: Rowan & Littlefield, 2004.

Holt, Peter and M. W. Daly. A History of Sudan from the Coming of Islam to the Present Day. London: Longman, 1988.

Jok, Jok Madut. Sudan: Race, Religion and Violence. Oxford: OneWorld Publications, 2007.

Hill, Richard. On the Frontiers of Islam. Oxford: Oxford
    University Press

INDEX